Uncommon Gratitude

Uncommon Gratitude

Alleluia for All That Is

Joan Chittister, OSB

and

Archbishop Rowan Williams

LITURGICAL PRESS
Collegeville, Minnesota
www.litpress.org

Cover design by Ann Blattner. Photos courtesy of Photos.com.

Permission for the following was in process at the time of publication: Excerpt from "East Coker" from *Four Quartets* in T.S. Eliot, *Collected Poems 1909–1962* (London: Faber and Faber, 1963).

ISBN: 978-0-8146-4905-3

5 6 7 8 9

Library of Congress Cataloging-in-Publication Data

Chittister, Joan.
Uncommon gratitude : alleluia for all that is / Joan Chittister and Rowan Williams.
p. cm.
ISBN 978-0-8146-3022-8
1. Gratitude—Religious aspects—Christianity. I. Williams, Rowan, 1950– II. Title.

BV4647.G8C45 2010
241'.4—dc22

2009045601

Contents

Growing into the Unknown

* written by Joan Chittister
° written by Archbishop Rowan Williams

INTRODUCTION

Someplace along the way, in the early years of my growing up, I heard someone explain that people who went to heaven would sit at the throne of God and sing "Alleluia" all day long. "Oh, no," I groaned inwardly. At that moment, heaven, however important it remained in my young mind, lost some of its immediacy, if not some of its luster.

Then, I grew up and realized the import of what it might really mean to be able to sing alleluia all day long, every day of your life. The very thought of it spun my world in an audacious new direction. What if life itself was meant to be one long alleluia moment? Here, indeed, resided the real meaning, the real hope, of life. But was it possible?

Years passed, however, before Archbishop Rowan Williams and I found ourselves agreeing to write a book together. We were both clearly marked by a monastic mindset that valued reflection above all else in the marketplace of spiritualities. Both of us took ideas as seriously as we took footnotes. God, we knew, was a mystery in which we lived every moment of every day. The only question is, How? What kind of a God is this God we seek?

Is God a teasing giant who must be pacified as we go through life? Is life an obstacle course designed to merit only the perfect, only the docile? Or is the human condition a bundle of gifts wrapped in darkness, the life task of which is to learn to recognize Goodness/Godness in all its misty forms?

One thing we were sure about: The presence of God in life required conscious contemplation. All the richness, all the manifestations of God in life could not be reduced to catechism answers. And yet, at the same time, in the God who was not amenable to simplification are all the answers a person needs to live a life full of confidence in what is seen, and also to take as a given the gifting of the unseen as well.

Finally, I asked him directly, "What really interests you most about the spiritual life?" He paused a moment. "I find myself coming back again and again," he said, "to the meaning of 'alleluia.'"

And then we were off. It took two days of thinking together in the archbishop's London office at Lambeth

Palace to find our way through to what we were both saying in slightly different accents: Life itself is an exercise in learning to sing alleluia here in order to recognize the face of God hidden in the recesses of time. To deal with the meaning of alleluia in life means to deal with moments that do not feel like alleluia moments at all. But how is it possible to say alleluia to the parts of life that weigh us down, that drain our spirits dry, that seem to deserve anything but praise?

The question is a worthy one. Life, after all, is a struggle, a journey in uncharted space, an exercise in both gain and loss, joy and sorrow. No life consists of nothing but success and satisfaction, security and self-gratification. Failure and disappointment, loss and pain are natural parts of the human equation. Then what? What use is an alleluia then, except perhaps to encourage some kind of emotionally unhealthy self-deception?

But alleluia is not a substitute for reality. It is simply the awareness of another whole kind of reality—beyond the immediate, beyond the delusional, beyond the instant perception of things.

One of the oldest anthems of the church, alleluia means simply "All hail to the One who is." It is the arch-hymn of praise, the ultimate expression of thanksgiving, the pinnacle of triumph, the acme of human joy. It says that God is Good—and we know it.

In the Hebrew Scriptures, the word is an injunction to praise, a call to the people to summon up praise in themselves. It is a challenge to see in life more than is seeable in any single moment and to trust it.

In the Christian Scriptures it is a formula of praise. Most of all, it is an intensely emotional response that, in early liturgical use, was said the entire year, as it still is in the Eastern Church, even in liturgies for the dead. In the most ancient part of the Christian tradition, then, it calls us to see all of life as life-giving, somehow, in some way, whether its present gifting is apparent or not.

Every segment of life is both gift and challenge, both endowment and responsibility. It is the warp and woof of the fabric we call time. The delicate interplay between the two has the power to rock us back and forth between total confidence and abject despair. We lurch through life between doubt and faith, between security and cloying uncertainty, between the enrichment that comes from differences and the divisions that come from fear. It is learning to cling to a sense of alleluia for both that carries us through life to that moment when everything in us has come to fullness and our only next step is immersion in God.

This book sees alleluia as a call to reflection, as the basis of contemplation, the final "Amen" to all that is, at whatever its cost to us now.

Archbishop Rowan Williams deals with scenes from everyday life with the eye of a realist who believes in God.

I, on the other hand, look at some of the defining moments those scenes imply and peel them back to discover what is under them of spiritual value and what is in them to take us to even greater spiritual heights.

The book is, then, a kind of dialogue between two people, both of whom are deeply involved in the urgency of pastoral demands but equally involved in understanding the relationship between what is now and what is meant to become in us in our private little futures.

It is an alleluia view of every present moment, a view that welcomes its complexity and subjects it to the more lasting view, the long view, of life.

To that, alleluia.

Joan Chittister

Discovering What We Are

FAITH

When the attack on New York's World Trade Center happened on September 11, 2001, it wasn't world politics that got global attention. Ironically enough, religion, not U.S. foreign policy, became the question of the age. As the Twin Towers came crashing down, the historical notion of the role of religion in the modern world crashed with them.

With three thousand of the country's most average people—file clerks and stock brokers, receptionists and department heads, accountants and computer programmers, office managers and corporation executives—dead in a single moment of radical violence, the message that chilled the country to the bone was the shout of the hijackers just before the planes crashed into the towers: "Allah be praised," investigators could hear the terrorists cry. It was the last sound on the cockpit recorder and it was jubilant, ecstatic.

"Allah be praised?" people gasped. What kind of religion was this that could find the wanton destruction of the innocent an act of religious praise?

Suddenly the role of religion in international affairs got more attention in the West than even God might have imagined for so private a subject in so self-determining a society. Proud of its position as a democracy in which the separation of church and state is a hallmark of its commitment to freedom of religion, America discovered that God was suddenly a major story. This was not the God of myth whose presence in life was reserved for moments of private prayer. On the contrary, this was the God of hard, cold news. And the news was not good.

After all, even the president of the United States, in one of his early statements to the nation following the attack on the Twin Towers, termed the attack by nineteen Muslim zealots from four Arab countries a "clash of civilizations." The underlying implications of such a statement were both startling and depressing. What exactly had happened to the world in those fifteen minutes of fury? Were we at a point where the God of the Bible and the God of the Qur'an were different divinities, each owned by one civilization or another? Were the divinities themselves now locked in mortal battle for the title of "The True God" or, at the very least, "God of the World"? And if so, what did that say about any kind of faith at all?

Most surprising of all, the whole issue was international news.

Papers that reported regularly on space probes to the moon, Mars, and Saturn, sophisticates in a technological world, were all asking the same questions, Is religion the answer or is religion the problem? In this situation, in our time, a religious question, decidedly unscientific, had emerged with startling relevance.

For the first time in the memory of anyone in the country, religion had become a more captivating topic than either political or international domination. News programs spent more time on the nature of Islam than they did on the political goals of any particular country in the Islamic world, let alone all of Islam at one time. Religion itself became the unknown enemy— not religious extremism necessarily, not simply religion gone rancid as it did, for instance, in the case of Jim Jones and the Jonestown suicides in Guyana, but religion of every ilk and stripe was now a question mark.

In the United States, religious extremists of our own began to talk about Armageddon, the symbolic final battle between Good and Evil, with a kind of glee. Televangelists warned people to get ready for the Rapture, to see the events both here and in the Middle East as part of the End Times.

More than that, however certain they were of the immediacy of the world to come, religious extremists of our own raised a banner of patriotism that supported everything from unsubstantiated, "preemptive" invasion of another sovereign nation to long-term imprisonment of unindicted suspects, secret prisons, and torture —all of them foreign to the history and ideals of a democratic nation. Violation of international accords as well as the abridgment of our own constitutional democracy became standard. Any amount of immorality became moral for the sake of preserving "the Christian world" from Muslim attackers despite the fact that we are more correctly defined, at best, as a nation the majority religion of which is Christian.

Clearly religious chauvinism had won the day over faith.

The problem, of course, is that both Islam and Christianity are monotheistic religions that spring from the same great line of patriarchs and prophets. Both say that there is only one God and that God is One.

And yet somehow, it seems, religion had managed to eclipse faith. When asked during this country's Civil War whether or not God was on the side of the North, Abraham Lincoln pointed out that it was not whether or not God was on our side but whether or not we were on God's side that mattered. In this case, that kind of theological unity seems to have slipped almost entirely from the national consciousness of religious extremists on both sides.

Instead, we were now simply two great religious armies arrayed against one another on the plains of the globe like giant football teams—whatever we said we believed about God. Whatever faith told us was true—that God was love and peace, justice and human community, that we were accountable for our behavior, that there would be an eternal judgment not based on political goals but on God's will for all humanity—religion told us was only really real for our side.

Clerics riled up the teams on both sides of the divide, promising God's blessing on those who would give their lives on behalf of the state. Suicide bombers on one side of the field carried scriptures promising instant heaven to martyrs. Military units on the other side of the field called civilian deaths, thousands and thousands of them, "collateral damage"—meaning "unfortunate," perhaps, but not morally reprehensible at all.

Religion defined what was going on from the vantage point of one side or the other, making God nothing but a tribal God. But faith tells us much more. Faith tells us that God is not the human political agenda writ large. God, faith tells is, is God—"that than which nothing greater can be thought," as a medieval theologian put it. God, in other words, is not amenable to either our expectations or the puny little human demands we call rational as we go our irrational ways.

God, faith tells us, is not the God of white people or brown people, of Pakistanis or Palestinians, of Jews or Catholics. God is the God of humankind who wishes "weal and not woe" to us all.

Yes, the attack on the Twin Towers caused large-scale death, but no larger in scale than the inadequately monitored chemical plant in Bhopal, or the British in Ireland during the famine, or the Americans in Vietnam fighting over territory not theirs. But it does raise a different kind of question. Why, we need to ask, has religion suddenly become such a major issue and faith such a subdued one? Why now and why here?

The answer to the question cuts to the core of the spiritual life. The fact is that it might well be that deep down we are still substituting a kind of magic for faith. God we make a cornucopia of human desires, a vending machine of human delights. We coax God to be on our side and call it faith. We cajole God to save us from ourselves and call it devotion. But those things reduce God to some kind of popular puppet. For those things there is little room for alleluia.

The truth is that faith requires the awareness that God is and that God is holding all of us responsible for the other. Being a card-carrying member of a religious tradition does not give us the right to consume the world for our own ends and in the name of God. We do not have the right to loose havoc on the rest of the world in the name of the God we have made in our own image. It is not getting the rest of the world to think and worship as we do that qualifies as real religion. It is giving ourselves for the welfare of the rest of the world to which we are called.

The Abrahamic tradition, in which Abraham's rush to welcome strangers to his table is one of scripture's most powerful icons, calls us all to be keepers of an open tent in the desert, for fear a stranger should simply happen to come by without water in the summer sun of the globe.

Faith is belief that God is leading us to become in tune with the universe, however different we see ourselves to be.

Faith is trust in the unknown goodness of life without demand for certainty in the science of it.

Faith is belief that the God we call "our God" is either the God of all or cannot possibly be God at all.

Faith is confidence in darkness, for the willingness to trust in the deep-down humanity of others as well as in our own may be the deepest act of faith we can possibly devise.

Faith is the willingness to see God at work in others —in their needs and ideas, their hopes and plans—as well as in ourselves.

Faith is the certainty that God is working through others just as certainly as God is working through us for the good of all humankind.

For those things we sing alleluia. Those are surely the only things that can possibly save the globe from our own unmaking of it.

Faith, real faith, real willingness to forgo our own need to either understand God's ways with humankind or control them ourselves, is real reason for alleluia. Why? Because faith is not about understanding the ways of God. It is not about maneuvering God into a position of human subjugation, making a God who is a benign deity who exists to see life as we do. Faith, in fact, is not about understanding at all. It is about awe in the face of the God of all. And it is awe that inspires an alleluia in the human soul.

Faith is about reverencing precisely what we do not understand—the mystery of the Life Force that generates life for us all. It is about grounding ourselves in a universe so intelligent, so logical, so clearly loving that only a God in love with life could possibly account for it completely.

When we center our power outside ourselves, which is of the essence of faith, we have faith in something greater than our smallness. We take our very lack of control as a sign of God's presence in the world. It is precisely because of our smallness that we can come to see and trust the greatness of God that surrounds us. It is only then that we can really come to see the face of God in the face of the other.

Faith in what we cannot control, do not see, cannot understand destroys the idol that is ourselves. It is only the deep-down belief that we are not the be-all and end-all of the universe that can save us from ourselves. It is the awareness of being part of something vast and intelligent and well-intentioned that gives purpose to life, that leads us to seek beyond the horizons of our smallness to the hope that tomorrow, warped as we may be today, we can all be better.

Faith in God is the only ground we have for faith in ourselves, in humanity, in life. Then we may care enough about others, about the purpose of God for all human life, to go beyond the kind of religion that turns God into a local deity and life into a zero-sum game in which winner takes all and losers abound.

Faith is one long alleluia sung into a dark night, the only end of which is another challenging dawn.

Doubt

The letter in my hand was written on pink flowered stationery and had a poignant ring. This was not a business-as-usual order, I realized, as much as it strove to sound that way. No, this letter broke life open to the core, and all under the guise of the mundane. "I would like to order thirty copies . . ." the letter began.

For a moment I had almost put the note down to mark it for transfer to the order department, sure that it had simply gotten to my desk by mistake. But on second thought I realized that the letter was simply too long, too personal, to be nothing but a purchase form. I went on reading.

Here was a woman, the writer said of herself, who organized book discussions for women in the area. They go to church, she went on, "but they find no one in any of them who will honor their questions." They are afraid even to ask questions, she said, because "when they ask a question they're treated as if they're heretics or have already lost their faith. Especially if they point out that the answer they get doesn't answer anything for them." Reading circles were the only way she knew, she wrote, "to help women find their voices."

Then she added what was not routine, even in letters of that sort. "I, myself, don't go to church. I'd like to be part of a praying community but I don't believe all the things they taught me anymore so I think it is more honest just to stay away."

I paused for a moment. No doubt about it: as a class, churches have been far better at giving answers than they have been at receiving questions. Catechism classes and Sunday School sessions, well-taught as they may have been, have been churning out routine answers to routine questions at regular age levels for eons. Unfortunately, the very age at which most people outgrow catechism class is exactly when they begin to grow into the spiritual confusions that are the essence of adulthood. Then the old answers begin to thin a bit.

For those for whom the questions persist, the choice is a bitter one: We can allow our spiritual lives to be capped in adolescence, assuming that faith has something to do with accepting childish answers to complex issues. Or we can follow our questions to the center of the mystery that stretches far beyond the theological politics of historical documentation. We can search to the point where only wonder will do or we can turn the spiritual life into some kind of corporate strategy aimed at storing up rituals in return for heaven. The one answer leads to the awesome undefinability of God. The other one reduces God to the exercises of a theological athletic field.

The fact is that all the great spiritual models of the ages before us found themselves, at one point or another, plunged into doubt, into darkness, into the certainty of uncertainty: Augustine, John of the Cross, Teresa of Avila, Meister Eckhart, John the Baptist, Thomas, Peter, one after another of them all wondered, and wavered, and believed beyond belief.

Surely, then, doubt is something to be grateful for, something about which to sing an alleluia. Unlike answers that presume the static nature of God and the spiritual life, doubt stretches us beyond ourselves to the guidance of a God whose face is not always in books. Doubt is what leaves us open to truth, wherever it is, however difficult it may be to accept.

But most of all, doubt requires us to reconfirm everything we've ever been made to believe is unassailable. Without doubt, life would simply be a series of packaged assumptions, none of them tested, none of them sure, and all of them belonging not to us, but to someone else whose truth we have made our own.

The problem with accepting truth as it comes to us rather than truth as we divine it for ourselves is that it's not worth dying for—and we don't. It becomes a patina of ideas inside of which we live our lives without passion, without care. This kind of faith happens around us but not in us—we go through the motions. The first crack in the edifice and we're gone. The first chink in the wall of the castle keep and we're off to less demanding fields.

Doubt, on the other hand, is the mother of conviction. Once we have pursued our doubts to the dust, we forge a stronger, not a weaker, belief system. These truths are true, we know, because they are now true for us rather than simply for someone else. To suppress doubt, then, to discourage thinking, to try to stop a person from questioning the unquestionable is simply to make them more and more susceptible to the cynical, more unaccepting of naive belief.

It is doubt that is the beginning of real faith.

The only real corrective for passive disbelief is passionate doubt. Our institutions are filled with people who never question whether or not the government and the Constitution are of a piece, whether our churches and the Gospel are compatible. So we produce unpatriotic patriots and corporate believers, people more committed to the system than they are to the following of Jesus. And we produce them at an alarming rate.

"Life is doubt, and faith without doubt is nothing but death," Miguel de Unamuno wrote. But in this case it is not the body that is dead, it is the mind, it is the soul. Worse, there is a complacency in untested faith that makes us vulnerable to the vagaries of change and disciples of a thousand idols. If God is still an old man in the sky for us, then to find not a hint of him in space exploration can be a real challenge to faith. If we never put our own beliefs to the test of inner truth, we are susceptible to every seller of intellectual schemes who stops us along the way. We become consumers of multiple falsehoods in our very desire for truth.

But doubt reduces complacency and leaves us open to larger, better explanations than the mythical ones we give to children until they are old enough to absorb the fact that God really is "pure spirit," however much we cannot imagine what that is, or how it can be, or what it means to the place of God in a material world.

The faith that demands explanations and "proofs" is not faith at all, of course. Faith is "things hoped for but not seen." But fortunately there is a bit of Thomas—the one who would not believe that Jesus was among them still without being able to touch his wounds—in all of us. There is a bit of the doubter in each of us who will not believe without seeing for ourselves that what is said to be true does indeed have some kind of truth to it, no matter how illogical, no matter how obscure.

Did this world make itself? Maybe—but hardly. Did I go through this illness alone? Perhaps—but in the midst of the depression of it, something outside myself sustained me, nevertheless. Has my hard life been without joy? Not completely—and sometimes, in the midst of the worst of it, I have known peace and strength greater than my own making. Have I never known the presence of God? No, in fact I have sometimes known it with consuming awareness.

It is at the point where we desire to see, because down deep our hearts believe what our minds cannot explain, that faith sets in. But the path to that kind of faith is only through the darkness of doubt.

There is simply a point in life when reason fails to satisfy our awareness of what is clearly unreasonable and clearly real at the same time—like love and self-sacrifice and trust and good. Data does not exist to explain these unexplainable things. Then only the doubt that opens our hearts to what we cannot comprehend, only the doubt that makes us rabidly pursue the truth, only the doubt that moves us beyond complacency, only the doubt that corrects mythologies not worthy of faith can lead us to the purer air of spiritual truth. Then we are ready to move beyond the senses into the mystical, where faith shows us those penetrating truths the eye cannot see.

Wealth

Singing alleluia for wealth does not sound, at first blush, as if it would be difficult. The fact is, however, that wealth may be one of the most demanding things in life for a person to handle well and really feel good about. My family, for instance, was certainly not wealthy, but I never knew it. We had everything we needed to enjoy life and even enough left over to give something to someone else. It was a nice balance.

Balance, however, may be exactly what the wealthy need to struggle for most of all. Or as the Chinese philosopher Hsi-Tang put it, "Although gold dust is precious, when it gets in your eyes it obstructs your vision." It is what wealth threatens to obscure that is the most important to be able to see. The wealthy go through life, for instance, faced with questions of balance on every level: When, exactly, is enough "enough"? And then what do you do with what's left over?

How does a person deal with the fear of loss that can come with wealth?

How can you separate your real friends from the ones who are just hanging around waiting for a handout? How can you tell who likes you as a person and who is simply there grasping for some of the reflected glory that comes with privilege?

How do you stop greed from eating you up and your whole world with it, as more and more of your life gets consumed watching the stock ticker or adding up the interest?

How do you save yourself from the excesses money provides and the emptiness that accompanies them? When what you buy doesn't fill the empty spot inside you, where do you go to deal with the shock such awareness brings?

To tell you the truth, I don't know the answer to any of those questions. After all, I never had to deal with them. But I have watched people in whom the virtue of money far exceeded the virtues that accompany poverty, voluntary or otherwise. For them, those questions are only incidental to the real issues that make the difference between being wealthy and being holy.

One of my first conscious excursions into the alleluia of money came in a conference in Asia where most of the participants were poor, the majority of them were women, and only a few of them were well-funded activist types or official observers. We were all there as some kind of professional analysts of women's issues around the world, but especially of the needs of women in developing countries.

The recommendations covered the usual gamut of needs that kept women everywhere in some kind of bondage to a money-driven world. They called for more education for girls in rural areas. They considered instances in which law itself bound women into some kind of domestic slavery and pointed out the necessity for more legislation geared to providing legal equality for women everywhere. They concentrated on the absolute correlation between the number of children per family and the poverty that arose out of the lack of birth control training. They argued for better health care programs for women, especially in times of pregnancy. Finally, they called for the participation of women at all levels of the political process in order to encourage and maintain the changes needed in the lives of women throughout their entire lifespan. We would now each try, we agreed, to get governments around the world to take these issues seriously.

It was a good conference and we were all very sincere. But it was what happened outside the sessions that gave me pause.

One of the participants, a Kenyan woman pastor of a Presbyterian church in Africa, simply passed the sign-up paper on to the person next to her at the table when it came around. The purpose was to collect people's e-mail addresses so the contacts and connections made at the conference could go on long after we left there. When they pushed the paper back to her, pointing at the line she'd left blank, Rose said quietly, "I don't have e-mail where I am. It is too expensive for us. And when I can use it, it is too slow to be reliable." She pushed the paper down the table again, and this time it made the rounds.

"I can't leave without seeing Rose before we go," a woman said to me later as we pulled our suitcases out to the cab. "I promised her that I'd give her something," she said, running back up the hostel stairs.

"What did you give Rose?" I asked her later in the trip. "My credit card," she said. "Your credit card?" I gasped. "Why in heaven's name would you give her your credit card?" I asked unbelievingly. "So she can pay for her e-mail every month," she said quietly.

The answer was a clear one. An alleluia for wealth has little or nothing to do with money at all. It has something to do with the way we deal with money, with what we do with it, with the manner in which we do it, with the reasons for which we do it. The conference would, in the long run, be very good for a lot of women. The credit card would make life better for at least one of them immediately. It demonstrated in a great glaring way the difference between talking about doing great things and doing what you can while you wait to do even more.

Clearly, the purpose of wealth is not security. The purpose of wealth is reckless generosity, the kind that sings of the lavish love of God, the kind that rekindles hope on dark days, the kind that reminds us that God is with us always. It creates in the holy heart a freedom of spirit that takes a person light-footed through the world, scattering possibility as it goes.

The only security holy wealth looks for is fruit of the good business practices it takes to keep on making enough money to give it away to those who need it more.

Most of all, perhaps, holy wealth brings in its wake the kind of simplicity that makes wealth a commodity to be shared rather than a product to be flaunted. The wealthiest family I know lives in a small cul-de-sac on the edge of the city in a ranch style house on a residential street. No great wrought iron gates here. No Olympic swimming pool in the backyard. No private plane at the airport. Nothing but a lifetime of philanthropy and good works, both private and public, both known and unknown, both great and small. It is the kind of wealth amassed to make the world a better place for all of us.

We sing alleluia to the wealth that invests in what can be—as well as what is. This kind of wealth seeds the hopes of tomorrow today. My favorite philanthropist is a woman whose heart is as broad as her soul, whose mind is as rich as her bank account, who has spent her entire life teaching her children to give away what hard work, privilege, and inheritance have given them. This is the kind of wealth that makes a social contribution that long outlives the life of the giver.

For this kind of wealth we all sing alleluia. There is no room here for resentment or smallness of soul. These are not people whose wealth we begrudge. These are people who show us that love is not dead, that God is not miserly, that unrequited love is possible.

They teach us what Seneca knew in the first century —that "a great fortune is a great servitude." It puts us in bondage to the needs of the rest of the world. Like the women in the Gospel of whom Luke speaks when he says that "[the women] provided for him out of their own resources," it gives us the power to do good. It is not the amount of money a person has that determines her or his real power; it is what that person does with it that measures her or his lasting influence in a society. Where force can only require us to do something, wealth can enable us to do more than we are. What greater alleluia can there be in the world?

Poverty

"I thank fate for having made me born poor," Anatole France wrote. "Poverty taught me the true value of the gifts useful to life."

There is something about such a position that fascinates me, I admit. But, if truth were known, I have never much appreciated this kind of talk about the poor by the rich. I live in a neighborhood where poverty, the capacity for barely getting by, and destitution, the daily struggle for survival, are too close too often for me to be able to tell one from the other.

Voluntary poverty, my kind, the kind practiced for centuries by religious groups as a kind of public protest against greed or as a model of Christian dependence on God and commitment to communal justice, is one thing. Forced poverty, the kind that comes despite hard, hard work in the face of the newly reemerging forms of unjust wages and contract labor, is entirely another.

The virtues of forced poverty, let alone some kind of alleluia for them, are likely, therefore, to escape me.

But then I heard a story. It seems that a very wealthy and socially active woman went to Bangladesh to see how she might be able to be of service to one of the most poverty-stricken areas of the world. At first, in the midst of such total destitution, the answer seemed obvious. But as time went by it became clear that the needs of the country were so great, so immediate, that the Westerner, however wealthy, hardly knew where to begin.

One obvious social problem was the condition of families themselves. The situation approached the desperate: too many women had too many children to care for and too many men had no land, no work by which to feed them. Family life in such a strained and futile and deprived situation had to be at a stage of interpersonal disaster as well as an economic one. But what to do about it?

She took to interviewing local people to get some idea of what they might need most. "What do you do where you come from?" a Bangladeshi woman finally asked her. "I'm a marriage and family therapist," the woman answered. "A what?" the local woman said. "I help people get through difficult periods in their marriages. Maybe it would be good if I did that here, too." The local woman paused a moment. "Oh, I don't think so," she frowned. "We don't have time to have marriage problems here."

I remembered when I heard the story that in Bangladesh they eat six pounds of meat a year and call themselves blessed. In the West, on the other hand, we eat 260 pounds of meat a year and call ourselves entitled to it. As a result, Western corporations go through the world cutting down other people's forests to get more grazing lands for us, and that means less farmland and fewer herbs for them.

Poverty, the grand act of staying alive in the midst of want, has a way, it seems, of prioritizing all the other problems of life and requiring its resiliency as well.

There is room for an alleluia even to poverty.

Poverty is what can make us grateful for everything we have. One new blouse does not get lost among all the other hangers in the cupboard. One new book becomes a treasure, not just one more kind of recreation. No new toys, no new clothes, no new furniture makes us treasure what little of each of them we do have. One mother I know found the pair of new shoes she had just bought her daughter that week in a bin in front of the house awaiting the city trash collectors. "What are these doing here?" she asked her daughter. "I just got them for you two days ago." "I don't like them," the teen said back. "None of the other kids wear anything like this." Only poverty, perhaps, can give us a sense of what it is to be grateful for what you have and even more grateful for what you get for nothing.

Poverty is also a well-worn road to humility. We know our place in the universe when we have barely a place at all. There is little to brag about here, even less to show off to others. We are thrown back simply on ourselves—on our personality, our character, our brains—when things cannot be what defines us. In our poverty we stand before the world stripped to the bone, "where life is sweetest," as Thoreau put it, with nothing to give, nothing to be admired for but ourselves. It makes a person dig deep inside herself to discover what of value she has that no one can ever take from her.

Imagination and inventiveness become the order of the day in a poor home. Adults sit in doorways and on porch steps and meet their neighbors as they go by. Children play golf with sticks and swing on ropes rather than sitting on cushioned settees. Poor people talk to one another rather than live with MP3 players in their ears. They learn to fish and play cards. They run basketball tournaments in the street because there is no basketball court in that part of town. They make a world in their minds and they live in it, without benefit of Nintendo games and Nikes, without office receptions and corporate banquets.

"He is richest who is content with the least," Socrates said, and Socrates may be far more right than the advertising agencies that create markets by creating desires. Desires unsatisfied, necessary or not, lead to a sense of emptiness in a society that measures value more by the number of things we stand to lose than the quality of the things we have inside us.

Most of all, poverty brings with it a spiritual vision the lack of which may in the end underlie the final corrosion of this wealthy society in which we live. Poverty stretches us to a vision of life that extends beyond the countinghouse, beyond the glutting of our lives with things. Poverty enables a person to see life in all its dimensions, to taste it in all its sweetness, and to recognize all its vacuousness. It enables a person to choose between what is real and what is not about a life lived in the midst of plastic and sparkles, of the lasting and the ephemeral, of the dehumanizing and the excessive. It reminds us of what is necessary and what is nothing but fluff, nothing but indulgence, nothing but consumption for the sake of show. Poverty keeps us real.

I do not applaud poverty or recommend it or justify it or minimize its struggles and its cruelty. I do not glorify the "happy poor." But I do see that a bit less engorgement and a bit more sufficiency in a society long ago surfeited and satiated by the unnecessary could, would, make the whole world richer. Then, perhaps, Bangladesh would have more meat and the West would need fewer marriage and family therapists.

In poverty, God is not a question. The God who hears the cry of the poor is all the poor can really be sure of because it can only be the goodness of God that supplies their daily needs. No one else does. Government does not. Industry does not. Only the graciousness of God in whatever form the day supplies does that.

To the poor a "good day" and a "bad day" take on different meaning than they do on Sanibel Island or Rodeo Drive. A good day is a day with enough to eat and a place to sleep for everyone in the family. A bad day is a day without what life requires to keep us sane, to keep us warm, to keep us from going to bed hungry.

For two-thirds of the world, poverty is the order of the day. Yet, as Epicurus knew, "Wealth consists not in having great possessions, but in having few wants." It is that kind of poverty of which Jesus speaks when he tells the rich young man to "sell everything you have, give to the poor, and come follow me." The alleluia that arises out of poverty is not about having nothing; the alleluia is in gratitude for the kind of poverty that wants for nothing that does not add to a sense of the presence of God and the liberating grace of enoughness. May we all be so lucky as to have that much. For that we must all shape our hearts in different, more life-giving ways. For that, we must all learn to cultivate in ourselves the poverty we do not know and grieve the riches that protect us from finding it.

DIFFERENCES

We are a people who herd. It may not be an image we like, given the association, but it's a reality, nevertheless.

When one family put in a rock garden on our street, rock gardens began to pop up all over the neighborhood. When one boy got shorts that hung to his ankles with pockets the size of saddlebags, every kid on the block showed up in them within two weeks. When the first school in the area began to require computers in the classroom, pretty soon they all did. We're a copycat society.

We grew up in national ghettoes called "ethnic neighborhoods" in a melting-pot world that never really melted. The Italians still ate Italian food, the Germans still had beer fests, the Greeks had church festivals, and the Polish still held street liturgies.

In grade schools everywhere kids ostracized blue-eyed boys one day and blond-haired girls the next for no reason whatsoever except that they had blue eyes unlike everyone else or blond hair unlike most of us.

Protestants lived in one part of the town I came from, Catholics lived in another.

Clearly, of all things unacceptable to the human psyche, the notion of difference may well be among the most threatening. We learn sameness very early in life and find it hard to stray too far from its boundaries, however old we get, however much we think we've moved away from such thinking as time goes on.

Sameness becomes a kind of security blanket that wraps us up in the warm feeling of being acceptable to the groups with which we identify and whose approval we seek. If we don't stand out, we can't be criticized. We are safe because we are just like everybody else. To be socially acceptable we have allowed ourselves to become socially invisible.

It is an effective technique, a kind of chameleon approach to life, but it is neither psychologically mature nor spiritually healthy.

Somewhere along the line we must become who we are meant to be as individuals. We are persons put on earth to contribute to it as well as take from it. Otherwise we doom ourselves to live a life that is only partially alive. Most of all, we must allow others to do the same, as much for our sake as for theirs. It is in the development of our differences that we thrive, that we are gifted by the presence of the other. It is in our respect for the differences of others that we grow. "Sameness," Petrarch wrote, "is the mother of disgust; variety the cure."

For the differences that make a person more than simply a carbon copy of someone else, we come face-to-face with another alleluia to life.

I remember having to grapple with the implications of differences as a very young Catholic middle-school child after World War II. As the child of a mixed marriage I had already contended with the great Catholic-Protestant divide and found it flimsy at best. But that was not so much "difference" as it was division. Now the whole question of what it was to be Jewish had exploded in the middle of the United States.

Jewish families, many of them refugees, all of them stunned and insecure in the aftermath of the Holocaust, found themselves a people within a people. They were "Americans" but not welcome members of American social clubs, for instance—not really part of the Gentile social world or the Christian religious world or the corporate business world. They were a people unto themselves.

But one of them stepped over the line. "Would Joan," the man wanted to know, "be willing to play with our daughter? We're Jewish, and Gentile children avoid her."

In that Jewish home I got my first experience of a universe outside my own. I began to realize that no matter how alike we might think ourselves to be, even in our own country, we were indeed different from one another. The only question was whether "difference" was a good thing or a bad one. In this "melting-pot" world of ours, of course, the message had been clear. We were all to homogenize into something beyond ourselves. Or better yet, "they" were to homogenize into us, the norm, the standard, the ideal.

But clearly it had not happened. I saw a mother light sabbath candles and a father say sabbath prayers, for instance. My mother and father never did that. Priests did religion where I came from. In church. Here, I learned, was a people whose home was their temple.

I read the little girl stories from her child's book of Hebrew stories and learned a part of the scriptures they never told me about in Catholic school.

I sat at a seder and learned to sing "Dayenu—It would have been enough" and learned to think differently about God's daily goodness to us. I touched the mezuzah on the door as I entered their home and learned to say a psalm verse as I did. I met their friends and went on family outings with them and learned that they did not eat pizza with ham on it or stuffed pork chops, the way we did, but they did eat bagels and lox and I liked those, too. In fact, I liked all of it. It changed me. It grew me in ways it took me years to completely understand, but grow me it did.

"When two do the same thing," Syrus wrote in his maxims, "it is not the same thing after all." We prayed and so did they, we celebrated feast days and so did they, we had a heritage—and so did they. Yes, we were very, very different in some ways, perhaps, but we were also very much alike. On what grounds could "difference," then, divide us?

The time spent so innocently with this quiet Jewish family gave me a glimpse into another whole world, and I found that world to be both benign and beautiful. It was a world that had things mine did not have, things that gave me new respect both for that community and for my own. It gave me an open heart.

Later, as the years went by, I made African-American friends who prepared me to understand Martin Luther King, Jr., and Russian friends who made me fear our own rabid anticommunism as much as I feared communism. Clearly there were people out there called "bad" by some, but who were, in fact, only different, not bad. And those differences enriched me.

Differences, I learned, were there to broaden us, to make us bigger people than we could ever have been had we stayed locked in our tiny little intellectual ghettoes. They make us think differently about the world. They make us ask questions about our world that cannot be answered on this side of that world's horizons. What else is education, in fact, if not an experience of differences that enlarges our perspective and increases our understanding?

The learnings that come from knowing the values of another people can easily reshape our own. The Arab commitment to family is a sign to the West of the dangerous extremes of rugged individualism. Here, where the whole concept of family is most in danger, most fractured by distance, most fragmented by mobility, the extended family of Arab cultures serves to remind us that personal connections are primary. In an increasingly fractured world, family is a lesson to be relearned, perhaps. In a culture of single-family dwellings and divided cities, it is at best a problem to be wrestled with, knowing that in the balance between independence and family may lie the key to world community in decades to come.

The new sense of self that comes from respecting the worldview of other peoples—about money, about moral standards, about social systems, about democracy—is both a humbling one and a freeing one. The West is not the center of the universe. Ours is not the only acceptable form of government or the only possible way of life. We do not have an obligation either to impose one or to avoid the other.

Differences not only teach us new ways of doing things; they also make us ask new questions of ourselves about what is really important in life, what really must have priority, what is really happiness, success, unity?

Differences are a challenge to our small assumptions about the way the world really goes together. An American world, a white world, a male world, a Western world are all simply small slices of reality attempting to be the whole. Only respect for the Muslim veil, the Chinese smile, the African tribe, the South American campesino can stretch us beyond ourselves, beyond a political imperialism that sets out to corrupt whole peoples in the name of globalization and, in the end, deprives us of the richness of the world community.

But that is the glorious burden of real Christianity: to follow the one who talked to Samaritan women and Roman soldiers, all the time allowing them to be who they were. Clearly, differences were not made to be homogenized; differences were made to be respected, to be honored, to be cherished. Alleluia.

Divisions

The problem became most evident with the election of George W. Bush, the man who promised unity and brought deep division not only to American society but to world politics in general. Friendly gatherings that had always been a kind of airing of national insights and political concerns suddenly, without warning, became a battleground of deep differences. People who before this period had been able to examine the policies of either a Democratic or Republican administration with a kind of critical objectivity and detached analytical concern suddenly became deeply partisan. Everything Republican was good, everything Democratic was bad. Or, conversely, everything Democratic was good, everything Republican was bad.

Worst of all, the differences were not political, they were "moral." These were not mere policies being discussed; this was a discussion, a position, on what was sin and evil and good and bad and freedom and totalitarianism and, underneath it all, fundamentalist Christianity and real Christianity, depending on who was defining what. Or, to put it another way, nothing in the United States has been the same since a handful of jihadists toppled the Twin Towers of the World Trade Center in New York.

Who "they" were, what "they" were about, and what should be done about "them," about us, about the world, about the role of the United States, about Christianity itself dominated every gathering, every institution in the country. We had become a nation under siege, a traditionally isolationist society with very global impact.

Families divided down the middle: friends found themselves on opposite sides of the political/moral divide. The rest of the world quaked at the conclusions being drawn as the sleeping giant roused itself and its armies to do battle against evil, to prevail in the struggle at Armageddon, to save the world from "an axis of evil" that was at best puny, however massive its intent.

In the blink of an eye, in the time it took to see the rubble smoke and cool, we had become a people divided, a globe divided. The famous picture of a band of boys braving the tanks in Tiananmen Square became a metaphor now for one body of people on the march toward an unseen enemy and another body of people standing in the way who were their own.

It changed conversations between friends. It put up social barriers everywhere. It left people alone in the middle of crowds that had always been safe harbor for them.

Who could possibly sing alleluia for the kind of disunity that shook families and friends, institutions and nations when nineteen young men of one stock managed to destroy what would easily have been seen by those of another stock as some kind of impregnable towers? What is there in that, that can possibly be seen as an alleluia moment? Madness, perhaps; a matter to be praised, never.

There are social answers to such questions. For instance, Alan Barth wrote, "Majorities, of course, are often mistaken. This is why the silencing of minorities is always dangerous. Criticism and dissent are the indispensable antidote to major delusions." But what about on the personal level? Where it hurts. Where it changes relationships. Where it takes some of the "family-ness" out of family.

Social division and dissent are alleluia moments in life because they make individuals of us all. We cease to be social clones when we care about something enough to articulate it differently than those around us.

It is, in fact, this very awareness of differences that gives us something to contribute to our world.

Going along, nodding yes to everything, keeping the norms, thinking by the rules never tests a concept; it only perpetuates it. So some people never drive a car, never use a computer, never leave their own country because the very thought of stepping outside the boundaries of their own experience threatens their sense of control. To go beyond our own comfort zone, our own experience is tantamount to stepping over the threshold of certainty. It leaves us vulnerable and exposed. It makes us a minority in a world where the majority, for the first time in life, perhaps, is not ourselves. It plunges us down into a place where it is not our language and our tastes and our ideas that are the coin of the realm any more. It makes us the different one whose differences hint of possible division. It makes us the outcast, the foreigner, the minority, the isolate.

It makes life both lonely and stultifying.

The truth is that it is only when we think against the mind of another that we find out what we ourselves really think, what we ourselves are willing to support. Anything else leaves us with colorless souls indeed. It is the sparks set off in us by the minds of those around us that fire our own. It is then that we become a real self. We become separate and connected at the same time. In the end, it is our relation to the ideas of the other that determines who we ourselves really are. To speak another truth, our own truth, our uniquely defined truth, however finished, however settled, is to confirm the value of our own existence.

Division of opinion, too often the fault line of human relationships, is, when we embrace it openly, what invigorates thinking and stirs new thought. It is the ground of new beginnings, the beginning of new insight, the foundation of new respect for the other. If anything sharpens the dull edge of a relationship it is often when it ceases to be boringly predictable. It is when everybody on two continents knows what we are going to say next that we know we have stopped thinking. Then we need to have a few old ideas honed. We need to think through life all over again. "Of two possibilities," my mother loved to tell me, "choose always the third."

Creativity, it is too often forgotten, comes out of differences. It is the ability to function outside the lines, beyond the dots, despite the boxes and the mental chains by which we have forever been constrained, that fits us to be the architects of the future. Instead, we want everyone to think alike when what we really need are people who are thinking newly—about theology, about God, about faith, about morality, about science, about life. "You won't find this year's birds in last year's nests," the proverb teaches, but we so easily miss the meaning of it entirely. Life is meant for moving on, the observation implies.

Just when we are most inclined to settle down, intellectually as well as physically, the folklore teaches, we are advised to remember that "steady" and "static" are not synonyms. It is one thing to move in steady step from one thing to another, respecting the best in each; it is another thing entirely not to move at all. We fail to realize that it is precisely the ability to think beyond the context of the times in which we live that makes us fit to live in times to come.

But we fear difference as the atrium to division. We do not like it in others because it threatens everything we have managed to understand and all that we have managed to do to this point. If these people do not come from a democracy, we figure, their notions of government are deficient. And then how shall we convince ourselves that their laws are just as good as ours?

If my God has always been an old man with a beard, I do not want to admit that there cannot possibly be any such thing if God is truly all spirit. It makes too many demands on my life: it makes feminine pronouns acceptable, even required, in fact. It makes the idea of God the Magician questionable. It makes old myths and old ways the things of spiritual childhood rather than moral adulthood.

We do not like different ideas in other people because they challenge our own vision and values. We need to know that we have not strayed from the realm of the acceptable into the realm of the possible, if for no other reason than that such meanderings off the beaten track tend to isolate us from the mainstream of the little intellectual islands on which we live. To bear the burden of a new idea in a society that does not want it can be the most excruciating life of all.

But if creativity is the natural child of division, critical consciousness is surely its only guardian. It is relatively easy to be different. It is far more difficult to be right. Bringing those two things together—the ability to think in creative new ways and the willingness to be self-critical—is the eternal salvation of any system. It deters the raw use of power and encourages growth. It frees us from stubbornness of heart—the never-never land of new thinking—for the task of stolidity of soul, of being able to entertain an idea until it has been proven untenable, not simply regarded as unacceptable. Critical consciousness is the testing ground of new ideas, the gatekeeper of tomorrow.

Being able to think differently from those around us and being able to function lovingly with people who think otherwise is the ultimate in human endeavor. It requires three things: a heart large enough to deal with conflict positively, enduringly, and kindly; a keen sense of personal purpose, the notion that there is something on the horizon that is worth debating; and a soul sensitive enough to transcend the tensions of the immediate for the sake of the quality of the future.

With the advent in the 1990s of neoconservatism and its avowed determination to turn the globe into an American village and business into a Western enterprise, the whole world has been brought to the moment of truth, to a choice between difference and division. Seldom before in society has any administration policy managed to draw an imaginary line in the sand beyond which persons could not go without rethinking everything they ever thought they could take for granted about life and how to live it in the name of God. It has been a moment of great challenge and deep personal renewal, perhaps in ways no church has managed, a challenge to bring the relationship between the spiritual life and the public life to the fore. Perhaps not since Jeremiah's vision of the sun shining freely over Baghdad as well as over Jerusalem have we been made to reassess our own place in the world so clearly.

In the end, of course, George W. Bush succeeded in garnering two electoral victories, both of them strongly contested. Through that entire era people struggled to find their own moral bearings, teetering as they went between two poles of a polarized society. They determined to continue to honor the system by refusing to be silent. They spent endless time stretching their own souls in an attempt to tell the difference between genuine conviction and bitter criticism. They thought through all their personal questions and public policies again. They struggled to maintain personal relationships that were strained by such completely contrary points of view. And in the doing of all those things they discovered the real meaning of the alleluia for differences. It was an alleluia for the time of clear thinking, for moral decision making, for conflict resolution and for reconfirming every value of a person's life.

It was not lost time. On the contrary. As Henry Ward Beecher put it, "God sends ten thousand truths, which come about us like birds seeking inlet; but we are shut up to them, and so they bring us nothing, but sit and sing awhile upon the roof, and then fly away." We learned to listen for the birds of difference on the roof of our hearts. And we became better thinkers because of it. Alleluia.

Conflict

The message, in essence, was a simple one: "We have no weapons of mass destruction," the Iraqi prime minister said into the cameras, "but, no, you may not inspect our weapons installations to see for yourselves."

People across the world began to take sides: some calling "crucify them," others, for all practical purposes, saying "touch not a hair on their heads."

The nations waited while the hair triggers of power were cocked and readied. Life would soon change for everyone, but who knew how much?

Millions of people marched in the streets, opposed to an invasion of Iraq. Others took over the airwaves, raising the decibel level of the moves toward war.

Many were intent on bringing patient planning to what had emerged out of the attack on New York's World Trade Center as an impulsive and brutal response to the wrong people at the wrong time. Equal numbers, with the faces of nineteen terrorists in their mind's eye, lost sight completely of the thousands who would be the targets of the kind of unjust justice they required.

Thousands of innocents would be made to suffer on both sides, the world knew, not for what they themselves had done but for what their governments did or did not do. Conflict would become conflagration and the heroes of the destruction, the people who endured the attack, would be the nameless dead.

World conflict, this opposition of enemies who have never even met, pits the guiltless against the unknowing, all for the sake of someone else's agenda and at the mercy of someone else's decision.

When conflict is on an international scale, those who are not the makers of the conflict bear the cost of the conflict. Those who design it reap the profits of it.

The debacle is called "liberty" and the world, by and large, goes its merry way, generally unmindful of the bloodletting let loose upon the soul of the globe for the sake of national vengeance or personal advantage.

When conflict is on the level of the personal, on the other hand, the results are the same, though hidden, internal, unnoticed publicly, but raging in the center of the spirit nevertheless. Here the war is waged inside myself where the pain is keenest and the private price can be high.

The soldier forced to leave home to destroy a people she has never seen struggles to find a reason for the carnage. The politician, informed only by papers someone else has prepared to convince him of his sovereign duty to destroy, finds himself conflicted about what patriotism really demands of him: to support this invasion or to resist it. The young wife, the new husband find themselves left to cope alone in what they thought would be companionship the rest of their lives. Community members, rejected and marginalized in their opposition to the struggle, feel the social ground shift under their feet as the conflict seeps into their bones, becomes a kind of emotional cement, and locks itself away unspoken and unresolved.

Conflict everywhere, at every level of society, threatens to swamp the heart and destroy the vision of the soul.

Conflict disquiets the universe, both personal and public. It goes on for years, deep in the innards of the human soul. The Holocaust continues yet in the minds of those who lived through it. The civil wars in Africa have spread their effects across Europe. Veterans of the conflict in Iraq still wake screaming in the night. Long after brutal husbands die, the women who bore their beatings still bear the marks on their psyches.

Learning to deal with conflict, learning to understand the benefits of conflict, determines whether or not peace can possibly be restored, even after the struggle is ended.

So what can there possibly be about conflict that we can regard with any kind of gratitude, any scintilla of alleluia? If we are not to risk sinking into a saccharine piety whose only answer to the suffering is that we must learn to "offer it up"—that we must learn to offer up our slavery, our festering wounds, our endangered children, our broken hearts—how can we possibly sing alleluia for this?

The warrants of conflict are, in fact, many—if we are willing to accept the responsibility for them.

The brink of conflict brings us all, nations as well as individuals, individuals as well as nations, to reexamine our best beliefs and our most pernicious responses to them. What kind of country, what kind of person do I really want to be? And is this really the way to become it? Will I be better or worse for not curbing my responses—the harsh words, the mean judgments, the snide remarks, the violent responses? Am I really helping the children by vilifying their father? On the other hand, am I really doing them any favor in the future by failing to let them know that he never paid a penny to keep them? Or in another arena, is the only way to destroy a dictator the destruction of the country we say we want to save?

Conflict confronts us with the test of integrity. It requires that we review constantly the arsenal with which we face our enemy. Is the spreading of enmity—the telling of lies, either national or personal, the undermining of trust, the spreading of prejudice—the toolbox of our trade? And, if so, how can the conflict, however reasonable, be resolved with any kind of integrity in the end?

The way we handle conflict brings us face-to-face with ourselves. It is we who are being tested for character in conflict, not the enemy, not the other.

Confrontation, to be successful, righteous, holy, must be based on respect for the other. We are brought to learn in conflict that we are not the masters of the universe. Others have a claim on it, too. If we enter into conflict with an open heart, we get a bit of perspective on the needs of the other, the arrogance of the self it takes to assume that all the needs are ours alone. Then, finally, we are given the opportunity to practice the fine art of de-escalation, of backing down from the high heights of holy righteousness to the point of a common problem.

Conflict both teaches us reason and taps in us an inner strength that nothing else on earth can either supply or confirm nearly so well. "Difficulties," William Ellery Channing taught, "are meant to rouse, not discourage. The human spirit is to grow strong by conflict." It is when we come out of conflict better human beings than when we went in, it is when our enemy comes out of conflict chastened, perhaps, but not destroyed, that we have learned what conflict has to teach.

Scripture gives us a model of both. Abraham refuses to destroy Sodom after routing it in his campaign to free his nephew Lot from its conquerors. Later, the king of Sodom seeks to make a deal: "You," he says to Abraham, "take the goods of the city and give me the people." But Abraham takes neither. "I will not have it said," he responds, "that you made me rich." Abraham seeks no vengeance on the people and refuses to profit from their loss. He has a clear mission—to free Lot—and he refuses to exceed it by reaping an unjust profit bred by the misfortune of others.

It is just such an attitude that proves the point of conflict. Any conflict. That difficulties must be negotiated in life is obvious. When the only resolution of a conflict is the complete humiliation or destruction of the other, we have long abandoned righteousness in favor of unmitigated power. But for conflict that leads to justice for both sides, sing alleluia loudly. It is the beginning of the reign of God.

Sinners

Well, for one thing, there are a lot of us around. . . . But yes; it probably does sound pretty strange to suggest that we ought to be saying alleluia for the existence of people whose lives are in contradiction to the purpose and direction of the universe as its maker intends it. That, after all, is what sin is. It isn't some sort of high-drama Satanic defiance, shaking your fists at the lightning. It isn't even exciting naughtiness. It's just the condition of being seriously wrong about reality and living against the grain. The committed sinner is the equivalent of the person who is convinced that you can make trains run on black coffee and is determined to go on trying, however much the evidence stacks up in favour of the more usual options. Sin is therefore bound to be, in the long run, deeply frustrating and, objectively speaking, very boring indeed. And on this basis, if you think about the devil, don't think of him as some heroic defender of moral liberty, but as a being tragically and pathetically locked up in delusions.

Now it's perfectly true that there's nothing to give thanks for about being wrong. But when someone says that they're a sinner, what they're saying is that they've noticed something is wrong. They have become an uncommitted sinner, to the extent that they know the world is bigger than their mistakes. It may not yet be clear how to get out of this situation, or even how to say anything clear or coherent about what's right; but it matters just to have some sense of incongruity between what's going on in your life and some overarching reality. It means that we haven't successfully got ourselves used to lying; and that is no small thing.

To say alleluia for sinners is to say alleluia for the beginnings of honesty. So much conspires to keep us more familiar with fantasy than truth. Take the immense energies devoted to promising technological solutions to human problems and the confidence with which we're still told that our current Western lifestyle is sustainable—the message that, in one way or another, every advertising campaign and every political campaign sets out to convey. Yet the obstinate suspicion is still around that we live in an environment of limited resource, that the degradation of that environment is more and more in evidence. A growing number of people are aware of an unreality, an incongruity, somewhere; they are, in Christian terms, waking up to being sinners. They're stuck with something they didn't choose or didn't know they'd chosen, and it feels false.

It isn't quite how religious people always use the term, granted. But if we forget for a moment the individualised and sometimes trivialised ways in which this language has been used and go back to the world of the Bible and the early traditions, we might see more clearly the importance of this central notion of being at odds with reality. When St. Paul talks about sin, it's obvious that he thinks first of a climate of thinking and behaviour in which we have become incapable of relating to God or each other except in fear, rivalry and suspicion, a climate in which we take it for granted that what's good for the other is likely to be bad for us. And Christian tradition has given us a formidable tool for diagnosis in the shape of the list of seven "deadly sins."

Once again, we've tended to treat these as a narrow list of things we shouldn't do instead of a sort of health chart or reality check. Is our behaviour characterised by arrogance, over-assertiveness? By jealousy, egotism, acquisitiveness? By obsessions about our physical needs or impersonal attitudes to sex? Is it shot through with a sort of apathy, emotional tiredness or deadness? These are the ingredients for unreal living, according to the tradition. If they sound familiar, and if they sound uncomfortably familiar, welcome to the company of conscious sinners—unreal people who yet haven't completely lost their taste for reality, who can still notice there's something gone askew.

An alleluia for sinners, then, is also an alleluia for people who are able to ask themselves awkward questions. If you know you're a sinner—that is, if you know that your perception of things is so skewed that you can't be confident of acting sensibly—you're that much more likely to be dissatisfied with some of what you're encouraged to take for granted about yourself or your society. Are these really the most important human needs? Is our way of life obviously what everyone in the world ought to want? Are these movements in the global economy inevitable and beyond challenge? The good sinner (if you see what I mean) doesn't necessarily have the answers; but she's very wary of dismissing the questions as silly.

In this sense, the "good sinner" actually lives in a larger, more mysterious, and more inviting world than the person who hasn't woken up, let alone the person who more or less deliberately refuses to wake up. I suppose that when we talk not just of sin but of evil, what we instinctively mean is the gap between the condition of recognising your own muddle and destructiveness and the condition of insisting that this is in fact how things are—or that it doesn't matter how things are, because what matters is only what I happen to want. Evil is not just inhabiting the cloud, the morass of unreality; it is affirming that it is good or normal or that the whole question is empty. It's fortunately fairly rare; but it's important to be able to recognise it. We see it in people who are incapable, it seems, of recognising hurt and humiliation to others for what it is. It's the mindset of the terrorist, the drug dealer, or the torturer, but we meet it in quite domestic circumstances too, with those who have no framework for seeing how they erode the life or integrity of someone else, in an exploitative marriage, in a situation of bullying in school, and so on. The point is not that we then have the right to say that these people are extra wicked and deserving of no compassion. It isn't about degrees of blame but about degrees of slavery to untruth. And for that there may be many reasons for which an individual isn't wholly to blame. It's very seldom that we really come across someone who has deliberately gone out of their way to turn the moral world upside down. What matters is that we recognise that here we are faced with a different level of resistance to truth—and that we don't have illusions about how difficult it is to change it.

In fact the good sinner will be able to spot the fact that his day-to-day prosaic actions marked by idleness, aggression, or suspicion are the soil on which a whole atmosphere of evil can grow. The small, barely noticed acts of self-delusion and self-serving have a relation to the pictures of horror—grinning faces around a humiliated prisoner, burning eyes fixed on the video camera as a hostage is butchered, blind denial of the facts of an epidemic or a famine because of political interest. Years ago, in one of the British daily newspapers, there was a satirical column that regularly featured a stupid and single-minded sociologist—"Dr. Heinz Kiosk," I think—whose invariable and automatic comment on any act of vandalism or brutality was, "We are all guilty." We can recognise the glibness of a certain generation of social commentators—but actually we shouldn't laugh too heartily. The sinner knows that the great evils of the world are not too hard to understand as extrapolations from much more ordinary behaviour; we need to be a bit cautious about using "evil" as a way of not thinking about someone else's actions, their significance and their origins—and their perhaps distant but very uncomfortable relation to more familiar patterns.

So the good sinner is aware of living in a bigger world than she can clearly see, and of being in some important ways a slave to illusions. She will be more than a little sceptical of whatever tries to silence her doubts as to whether the familiar world is, after all, the natural and obvious one. She will have noticed that there is some quality of relationship missing from her life. There will be a certain amount of shame and self-dislike around, because of this sense that somehow the usual pattern of actions and reactions isn't free but follows a whole agenda of instinctive and compulsive or habitual moves which don't fit too well with the recognition of what's possible. St. Augustine has had a bad press for what he is supposed to have said about sin, but at least one line of his has always made me think he has been unfairly treated. When his opponents tried to maintain that every sin was a fully conscious act of rebellion against God, he replied that most sins were "committed by people weeping and groaning"—people who knew better and felt trapped. It's one of the most realistic and compassionate insights in early Christian literature.

The sinners I appreciate are the ones who look at their situation and ask, "How did it come to this?" Here are people I love or at least care about a bit—yet I seem to have damaged them, and to go on damaging them. Here is a plan that began with high ideals, and now it's bogged down in compromises and failures. Unless I choose to pretend that all's well, I have to ask, "How?" A sinner who has woken up is someone who knows he has some learning to do, who knows at least a little bit what to do with the time left. It's not straightforward, and we're not going to learn what we ought to learn by our own resources according to a tidy plan (which would just get us back to where we started). But the important thing is that bewilderment about how we got here and the sense of the world being bigger and stranger than my planning mind.

It's what an earlier generation would have called humility. Yet again, the word has been almost ruined. The pictures it calls up for us are of hypocritical and exaggerated ways of putting yourself down—of being passive in the face of injustice, or of so distrusting yourself that you won't take adult responsibility or risk making a mistake. But the questioning I've been trying to describe is anything but passive, and it needs the most difficult kind of responsibility. It means that I take responsibility for my integrity, that I go on examining my relation to the truth when it would be more comfortable (on the surface, anyway) not to. Humble people can start revolutions.

Rosa Parks died quite recently, the black woman who refused to give up her seat all those years ago on a bus in Alabama: the incident that really sparked the final and greatest phase of the civil rights movement. She was a humble person, even dare we say it, a good sinner. She knew that she was caught up in a system of unreality, not by her fault or choice; she knew that she ought to be asking a question about it; she knew that there was, all of a sudden, a choice about whether she would let daily absurdity and injustice go unchallenged. And she was too tired to argue with her intuitions. She took her responsibility because, as a good sinner, she knew that whatever in her life was marked by a selfishness or idleness she could change if she wanted was somehow connected with the evil of the world around—and that therefore there was a possibility, an extraordinary possibility, of acting as if that evil was not the last word. If she could decide about something no one expected her to decide about, what might become possible for others? She didn't know, and I don't for a moment imagine that all this sort of thing went consciously through her head—but she acted as if the world was bigger than she or her society had thought.

That's humility; and humility is also to be heard in the voices of those who protest about corrupt practice in industry, whistleblowers in any institution, people who say, "Stop; no one can be trusted with this sort of unaccountable power, no one has the right to protect themselves like this." It is the radical voice that comes from knowing we all have to go on learning. It is a sort of self-distrust—but not the corrosive kind that says, "I'm not worth trusting"; it's more the kind that says, "I know my limits; help me stay honest." And to others it says, "Don't hide from yourself what you may become if you forget the truth." Humility like this doesn't make the world drab and dangerous, something to be avoided because it's all too difficult. It uncovers a world that is dangerous all right, but one that has to be explored and learned about. Without that learning, we shall be stuck in a pinched and dull version of reality.

Humility ought to be the gateway to excitement, the excitement of precisely that grown-up sense of the world which is ready to make and to acknowledge mistakes for the sake of moving out into new depths. The good sinner is humble because he knows how much that exploration will be capable of getting distorted by the falsehoods he has taken in without noticing and that have become habitual and comfortable. But he knows that the refusal to grow and learn is to be condemned to what are, in the long run, worse risks.

Somewhere in the middle of it all is the buried awareness or half-awareness of that broken relation from which it all flows—that element in us that makes fear seem rational and natural when we look at each other and God. And we don't really get beyond this, of course, unless we have a glimpse of what a relation might be that wasn't like that. We need the tightening circle of our unreality to be interrupted by something quite strange. It's interesting that, for a lot of people, being faced with a serious work of art, a play, a really good film, or a piece of music, is one of the things that gives them a clue about what humility means; here, faced with this strange gateway into another way of seeing or hearing, I know my world is too small and my life is inadequate. It's not that I suddenly get to hate myself or doubt my worth—indeed I may have a stronger sense of worth because of this. I just know that my frame of reference is put rather harshly in perspective when it's brought into the light of a greater imagination.

This is actually rather obvious when you think about it. If our world of suspicion and smallness were never interrupted, we'd never have reason for thinking it wasn't the whole story. We could live securely—if not very happily—in our version of reality if the truth didn't leak in from time to time, whether through someone's life or a work of art, or just (for many people) the experience of solitude and silence, when we can't avoid the sense of bad fit with the truth. The good sinner, or what I called the uncommitted sinner, lives in a world she knows to be leaky; something unsettling is always finding its way in.

This helps a bit in seeing how Jesus makes a difference in the Gospel stories to the world around him. When he's there, people see themselves differently. Remember Peter, when Jesus has told him where he can find a miraculous catch of fish? He simply says, "You need to be away from me, sir, because I'm a sinner." Miraculous generosity is there in front of him—and all he is sure of is that this isn't the climate in which he lives. Only Jesus is quite clear that it's time he started. The same with Zacchaeus, the little tax collector who climbs the tree to see Jesus, hoping he won't be noticed. When Jesus stops and turns his face upwards to look at him, he doesn't say, "You're a sinner, you need to change your ways." He doesn't need to. He just invites himself to Zacchaeus's home and Zacchaeus at once says, "I'll have to be different."

Peter and Zacchaeus are seeing for the first time an authentically human face, one that isn't distorted by fear of God or other people. And that's all that's needed. If there can be a face like that in the world, just the one, the world I know is too small. So every time Peter or Zacchaeus or you or I say, "I'm a sinner," we're reminding ourselves of the glimpse given through Jesus of the real world we'd never have dreamt of, left to ourselves. A pretty good reason for an alleluia.

Because this recognition of being a sinner carries with it the confidence that there really is a way out. From our point of view, it's a slow process, full of frustration, two steps forward, one step back, fresh illusions and so on. But the point is that God has thought it worthwhile to interrupt directly—to show us what the scale of our problem is and to offer a relationship that will hold us, however shakily from our side, in the truth. Christians have spent a fair bit of energy trying to sort out exactly how this works; they know it is rooted in the death of Jesus, the moment when the world's preference for unreality seems to win decisively, yet also the moment when God's truth is in fact the winner—but they haven't found one simple way of explaining it. That's all right. The alleluias come first. Alleluia for the interrupted life that mercifully lets me know I'm wrong and that my wrongness can be dealt with; for the tearing of a veil and the vision of a landscape.

Saints

Actually the same people are sinners. Not just in the obvious sense that every saint starts as a sinner, that is, as an average mess of a human being; but also in the biblical sense, the sense in which St. Paul calls the people he's writing to "saints," when they're clearly just the kind of shambolic failures we recognise rather easily. Being holy for the Christian isn't some kind of a characteristic along with others ("she was short, fair-haired, overweight, and holy"). It's something to do with being in a particular kind of relation to God that allows certain things to happen.

If holiness were a characteristic like others, some might have more, some less; and you might either be envious of another person's holiness ("I wish I had fair hair and holiness like her"), or set out to acquire holiness by effort. The awful paradox about holiness—which is why I should probably stop writing this chapter right now—is that the harder you try and the more self-conscious you get about it, the more massively unlikely it is that you'll get the point of it, never mind sharing it. To use a rather overworked metaphor, holiness is as little a characteristic of a person as light is of a window. Put the window in a particular place and the light comes through; put a person in a particular place and God comes through.

God comes through. It's the difference between saying someone is really good and saying they're holy. The good person, whether by temperament or by effort, is someone who does what's right and constructive and sensible. Sometimes such people can have an unaccountably depressing effect on others; they make you feel that little bit worse about yourself. The holy person, by common consent across the centuries, is someone who enhances the world for others, who generates joy—not by a great effort of cheering people up (God forbid), but just by being themselves. If you think back for a moment to the last chapter, you might compare them to works of art—they simply tell you that the world is bigger.

So when I think of holy people, my first thought is of those who have made me see more. Sometimes they have been conventionally saintly, sometimes not. Some of those who quite clearly open the doors of vision are very flawed persons, with deep-seated problems or compulsions—Martin Luther King, Jr., is probably the best-known example, but I can think of a good few others in my own experience who have genuinely had this "something else" about them that doesn't seem to be cancelled by weaknesses of temperament or habit, by sexual complexities or trouble with alcohol or whatever. To say that such people can be in an important sense saints isn't to say that their weaknesses or failures don't matter or that they're not really weaknesses at all—and the people in question certainly wouldn't want that said of them. It's just that they are constantly and courageously standing in a place where the light comes through.

But as for the more "conventionally" holy: a lot of people read Tony Hendra's wonderful book, *Father Joe*, when it appeared a couple of years ago and discovered there an example of holiness that was utterly without sentimentality or religious flannel. What the book does is to show someone whose surprised and delighted attention to everyone who happened along managed to convey to each one that they were uniquely interesting and loveable—or rather, that they were not "uniquely interesting and loveable" in virtue of being extra special, but that simply because they were there, because they were human, they deserved interest and love without reserve. I had the great blessing of knowing Father Joe myself over many years, and the holiness I experienced was simply that confidence that nothing would be rejected or dismissed, everything would be taken seriously, that what I said and thought and struggled with would be heard and then somehow given back in a new pattern. I've said that you would be taken seriously; at the same time, you would emphatically not be encouraged to take yourself seriously in the wrong way. And when I went once to him to try and sort out a painful trauma that had left a great sense of failure, I began to understand what compassion really was: I was heard with a pity and tenderness that didn't make me revel in being a victim, but taught me to see myself with a realistic tenderness that then had to be passed on to others.

Alleluia for this, and alleluia on behalf of all the others who learned it from Joe. The saint is someone who starts a chain reaction of new perception in the world, who reinforces, even among those who don't or can't yet believe, the confidence that there's more to us all than we have suspected. And this doesn't necessarily go with a temperament that is so self-effacing that you'd never notice a saintly person in company. Here's a common enough mistake, imagining that selflessness is the same as a particular kind of temperamental meekness or unobtrusiveness. Happily, saintly people come in all varieties of temperament, so that it doesn't matter whether you're depressive or extrovert or irritable or whatever. I've met genuinely holy people who have indeed been naturally self-effacing, saying little, gently refusing to be drawn into the ordinary currents of social exchange. I've also known people like Desmond Tutu, whose best friends could not claim he was self-effacing. If Joe taught me something about real and truthful compassion, Desmond taught me a lesson about the possibilities of a kind of holy egotism. There are some people who so enjoy being who they are that they make everyone else in their vicinity enjoy being themselves—the exact opposite of that more familiar egotism that pushes others into the background so that the star can be centre stage.

It's because I associate holiness with this sort of altered perception, I suppose, that I don't think it can be spoken of as a characteristic of someone, let alone as just a kind of intensified goodness. It's always active, it seems. It alters what can be felt or thought or done, and it does so not by strategy or effort but by being itself, being a window. If this sort of vision or tenderness or integrity is possible in that life, isn't it possible for me? Which is why saints are hated as well as loved. The Gospel of John already sets out with chilling precision the mechanism by which untruth fights back against its exposure;

holiness makes things worse as well as better. "If I had never come and spoken to them," says Jesus in one of the most haunting verses of the Gospel, "they would be free of sin." His presence has provoked a crisis, a choice: for or against? The new world or the old? You can't be innocent any longer; you have to be either awake to sin and forgiveness or deliberately blind.

Jesus is for Christians the one human agent who never blocks out the light, whose life and presence define holiness in each moment. But the saints who gather in his company and try to stay faithfully in the place he occupies are, as we have seen, flawed in various ways, and vulnerable. What a relief it is to see that such and such a person is flawed! Perhaps after all we needn't take them seriously. How many people were secretly relieved when Martin Luther King, Jr.'s, private life came to light; at last we can patronise or condemn, we needn't feel at a disadvantage or sense that we ought to change. In different degrees, that sort of relief is at work every time someone attempts to "deconstruct" a great figure. Even straightforward failure helps: it was a wonderful dream while it lasted, but now we see that this isn't the real world after all. We don't have to be upset by alien possibilities.

It makes me wonder occasionally whether after Good Friday the disciples of Jesus, in the middle of their grief and terror, didn't feel a touch of relief; it makes me understand better why some of them really didn't want to believe in the Resurrection.

Holiness is what happens when someone is knocked off balance by the reality of the new world; and to see that is to see something that is both hugely frightening and hugely exciting. Thomas Hardy's poem about the old country tradition of the animals kneeling down in the fields and sheds at midnight on Christmas Eve shows us a sceptical, world-weary author wanting to go and see, "Hoping it might be so." And the hope persists. People do, it seems, want to read about Father Joe and similar figures; they hope that there is a window somewhere into a vision that isn't just an idea but a powerful, nonnegotiable fact. Yet if Thomas Hardy had really seen the oxen on their knees, would he, by Boxing Day, have found a good reason for sticking to wistful agnosticism?

Holiness is something we want and don't want, something we long for and dread—exactly as the Bible spells out the way human beings relate to God and react to the coming of God in a human life. Jesus casts out a spectacularly destructive devil—and the local people beg him to go away. He promises unconditional mercy and welcome—and is crucified. In other words, holiness is a reminder, once we start thinking about it, of all that we and our whole human history have done to make us allergic to reality, but also of the fact that we've never managed to extinguish the longing for it.

Alleluia for saints, for people who are ready to carry the cost of standing in the light, even when the light shows up their own inadequacies and oddities. Someone discussing the great nineteenth-century English prelate, Cardinal Manning, objected to his being called "saintly"; surely he was a manipulative, ambitious, even unscrupulous figure. But another scholar replied that the miracle wasn't that a saint could be manipulative, ambitious, etc., but that a man with a temperament like that could in some sense still be a saint. The undeniable fact that he let God's light come through for countless people, especially in his selfless work for the poorest workers in Victorian London, certainly makes his less attractive temperamental qualities very evident by contrast. But what matters is that at some level of his being he was knocked off balance by the reality of God's love and justice, and that reality was simply there in his life, never mind the intrigues and the rivalries of the church politics he was involved in.

We're supposed to live in a tolerant and permissive cultural climate. But—if the way the popular media works is any guide—we also have a powerfully moralistic and judgmental streak; we expect (or at any rate pretend to expect) that good people are just good and bad people just bad. We don't cope well with the complexities of people's lives. Celebrities and politicians (who are now a sort of celebrity) are dressed up in various sorts of myth; they are presented as good, simple, honest souls, then reinvented as villains or pathetic victims, then restored to popularity, with the embarrassing stories forgotten. It's difficult to distil from this any sense of a single life, with good and less good elements, with mistakes and betrayals, shame and sorrow, recovery, self-knowledge. Life becomes a succession of disconnected tableaux. And that isn't an easy climate in which to understand what a saint might be. If, as I've been trying to suggest, a saint isn't simply an extra good person but a person who has learned how to live in a particular place so that the light comes through, we ought to expect most of the saints to be pretty uneven, not to say confused characters. If they combine transcendent spiritual presence and insight with a degree of vanity, cowardice, authoritarianism, or other doubtful features, it doesn't invalidate the insight. They are not there to tell us that we can be as good as they are if we try really hard; they are there to tell us that if we hang around in their company long enough, we may with them get a feeling for that other world where change happens not by effort but by absorbing love.

So if we go back to the Bible and to St. Paul in particular, we can see why the word "saints" appears there in a sense that isn't quite what we might expect. The folk that Paul writes to are not extra good; they are simply people who have come to live in the vicinity of Jesus and to breathe the same air. It makes their failures and betrayals all the more evident; it may even at times push them into more extreme mistakes. And it doesn't make them automatically popular with those around—or even automatically better able to get on with each other. It's just that they are awake; they can't pretend the world hasn't changed. They've made themselves responsible for making this new world visible and believable.

You can see what I mean, I hope, by saying that they're the same people as the sinners—people who challenge what seems obvious in the world. Like the artists with whom they have a lot in common, they keep the doors of vision open when everything and everyone seems to want to close them. And once you have been in this territory, you know that you have to start afresh, and that what you thought was possible has been a good deal enlarged.

The Church makes quite a business of declaring who is and who isn't a saint in official terms, and I suppose there is a good deal of sense in having a sort of minimum list, as if to say, "When we say 'saint,' we mean people such as these." But we need to beware of two possible blunders here. One is to imagine that once someone has made the official list it is impossible to ascribe serious errors, sins, or failings to them. Inhuman paragons don't help us; what we need isn't people who are at the top of the class in Being Good, but people who show us the glorious and troubling difference of God. And the other mistake is to think that sanctity is restricted to the official list. We all have personal lists if we think about it, lists of those who have made God real. It doesn't hurt to have our own calendars of commemoration for such people who may be famous public figures or just people we've happened to know. And I've sometimes thought it would be a good idea for parishes to have that sort of commemoration of those who have really opened the doors for a local community. Imagine the parish newsletter: "This week: 4th October, St. Francis of Assisi; 5th October, Thelma Russell and Pete Corcoran . . ."

Which also reminds us of the essential fact that holiness isn't often a matter of great public acknowledgement and popularity. There is a hiddenness to it; we should expect most saints to be known to relatively few people for what they are. If you want to put it in rather dramatic terms, it's one of God's most successful strategies against the powers of evil: God's work goes unobserved. In C. S. Lewis's novel *That Hideous Strength,* the diabolical villains are in most respects diabolically clever—especially when it comes to exploiting people's weaknesses. What they are completely useless at is spotting where the real opposition to their plans will come from. The holy people in this book are the ones the villains don't notice or think are too boring to worry about. There is a very ironic passage where the evil characters are trying to identify those who are going to give them trouble, and they settle on one man who is very prominent in church politics and very up-front about his religion. But this man in fact plays no part in the book; we don't even meet him. The real work is being done by someone else.

An alleluia for saints means an alleluia for the people who get the work done, the work of letting God through. There's a popular hymn about the saints which has the line, "We feebly struggle, they in glory shine." The obvious meaning is that the saints have made it, and we're still on the journey. But I like to think that it has another meaning. In God's eyes, the people who shine with glory aren't by any means always the ones who seem to make the most noise working and struggling and battling. Those of us who are caught up in all this sort of action or activism need to remember that the actual work is probably being done by someone we'll never meet or know about, someone whose ordinary life so shines with God for those around him or her that they make possible new things I couldn't dream of. Of course we still do our best, and we don't use this conviction of the work being done somewhere else as an excuse for sitting on our hands. But it gives us a sense of proportion and patience; it makes our own blunders a little more bearable; it even helps us see that the way we do what we have to do may make a difference somewhere else.

There are no straight lines of cause and effect where holiness is concerned. It's more the case that God uses whatever space we make for whatever God has in mind, wherever it may be possible. All that counts is that some people are so knocked sideways by God that they make space for the divine life to come through and that they stay there where God has met them, with God's action and life pouring through their own confused and very human hearts and minds and bodies, letting the face of the earth be renewed.

Becoming Who We Are

Genesis

I am unreasonably proud of knowing exactly where my mother's family lived from the eighteenth century onwards; it's still possible to identify the couple of fields they owned in Llanddeusant in Carmarthenshire, and the small farmhouse on the other side of the mountain in the upper Swansea Valley where they spent most of the nineteenth century. And on my father's side, there is the immense family Bible in Welsh with the pages at the beginning for the birth, marriage, and death entries. It tells me where his family was in the nineteenth century and it reminds me of some harsh historical truths about mining families of the period when it records the deaths in infancy of two of his eight siblings and of his mother when he was seven.

Unreasonably proud, because in one sense knowing your family history doesn't seem obviously useful or significant. Yet people are still fascinated, even obsessed by it, all the more so as the routine ways of record keeping fade from memory (you don't see many family Bibles around these days). We need, apparently, to be able to put our lives into a larger context, a longer story, recognising that we can't really tell our own stories without involving this bigger perspective—and that there are things I shan't understand about myself unless I look further. This needn't be a matter of searching for deep psychological currents or compulsions, family curses or family genius, but just the sense of what made my parents who they were, what sort of things made them hopeful or afraid, what they saw out of their windows (literally and metaphorically), so that I can see better what they were passing on to me before I was conscious of it.

Sometimes, both in individual lives and in the lives of societies, this process of rehearsing your story is a form of self-justification or self-defence, a means of justifying once and for all why we are where and who we are as the right way to be. Here, we say, is a history of success, or of courage against odds, or of persecution and injustice; we have to hold fast to what was won with such difficulty, or we need to keep up the standards of our noble line, or we need to seek reparation for the injuries we have received. We do this, we are like this, we have these claims, because of all that has gone before. We can't be expected to change. This is the way things have happened and it can't be argued with. Yet from one point of view, of course, this is a rather odd approach to the matter. When we tell a story, we can't help indicating the different ways things might have gone: we ought to come away from our storytelling struck by the sheer chanciness of what happened, aware that it didn't have to be like that. Good history isn't the unfolding of foreordained, necessary patterns, but the tracing of all the diverse and unexpected factors that made things go this way rather than that—which is why the "what might have happened" game (what if such and such a battle had gone the other way? what if so and so hadn't accidentally fallen off his horse just then?) is enjoyable—just as it is in our individual lives (what if I hadn't gone to that party and met you?).

We need to know where we come from; and we need to be aware that it's a story that will show us at every turn that some things could have been different. For this reason too, history can be a good way of letting us know how much now depends on both choice and chance; it can help us to a realistic awareness of how decisions matter in ways we can't control or grasp. It tells us that we are free to make a difference, but also that we don't often know just what the difference will be.

So it's natural that the Jewish and Christian story begins firmly at the beginning. "Genesis" is a word that means "becoming" in Greek; this is the book about how we became the way we are. The Bible itself starts, you could say, as a family Bible. But one of the most striking things about the book of Genesis is that it isn't a story of ancestral triumphs, a record composed to justify where its authors have got to; it suggests that our history both as a human race and as a community of God's friends is a history of misunderstanding ourselves and our needs and desires. Instead of pointing us neatly back towards a golden age in the ancestral home, the story is one of repeatedly leaving home. As soon as there are conscious beings around in the world, they leave home—or rather are expelled from home because they have tried to get what human beings can't get, instant knowledge and invulnerable life. In their exile, they continue to fail, so dramatically that the whole earth is taken away in the flood and the human race is made to begin again. Abraham, the ancestor of God's people, is uprooted from his own home and sent on a long and circuitous journey to somewhere else. He is asked to sacrifice his son, as though his family will not after all inherit what he has been given, as though the whole of his journey and quest has been a nonsense. And when his descendants seem almost settled in a land they can call their own, there is an unplanned mass migration to Egypt.

This is a very strange way to write a book of beginnings or becomings. It hints very strongly that life as a human being, even as a human being befriended by God, is a life where growth always means a step beyond what is familiar, a step away from home; that "exile" is a state of being for us. The further back we look at our story, the more clear it becomes that we are, in one sense, never at home. Or rather, being at home is a matter not of settling down for good somewhere, in a place beyond questions or growing; it is something to do with a fundamental trust in the God who accompanies us in our travelling. Because the other great theme that runs through Genesis is "covenant"—the repeated promises made by God, to Adam and Eve, to Cain, to Noah, to Abraham and his family. Whatever happens, however they have ignored or offended against what God asks of them, God commits to being there alongside them.

Genesis in its present form was put together at a stage of Israel's history when the experience of exile was still vivid. A new generation of literary and legal scholars was putting together a book that would express what they saw as the heart of the people's identity in relation to the God they served, the God they believed had called them. With the recent experience of disruption, of absence and return, fresh in their minds, they had an agenda to fulfil. And from the mass of tradition that confronted them, they pinpointed those elements that most clearly echoed these recent memories of life in an alien culture and the unexpected difficulties of settling back in an environment that should have been "home" and yet felt deeply strange.

In God's company, every supposed homeland is strange: God is never to be contained in a landscape, becoming familiar and comfortable as the view from a bedroom window. God is a homeland when everything else is strange and hostile, the one factor in the situation that is never altered by circumstances. God does not have an ancestry, a process of becoming: all we know of God is what God offers to be known in the promise made, the freedom of God to be always there accompanying the ones he calls. If God summons Abraham from Mesopotamia (just as he recalls the people of Israel from their exile by those far-off rivers), God is also waiting in the new landscape, on the unfamiliar hills of Palestine, to meet him there. Home is God's company: something that can only be discovered as the history of disruption and exile unfolds.

It is a perspective that casts a new light on the idea of the "promised land," so significant in Genesis and Exodus. The narrow strip of country from the Golan to the Negev is the background against which all this is worked out, a place to which the characters of the history return in their constant wanderings, which is a sign of God's faithfulness: this is where they will always meet him, because he has set there the imprint of his "name," his presence.

As the theology of the Hebrew Scriptures unfolds, the city of Jerusalem and the temple become the marks of divine presence and involvement. Whenever the people assemble in the land and at the shrine, they will recognise the God who has been alongside them once again, the God of their ancestors. Yet there is no simple storyline that will lead the people into a happily-ever-after possession of this territory; when they settle there and forget God's requirements, they have already spiritually become exiles from the company of the God whose land it has become. Both Christians and Jews have at times entertained some strange beliefs about the land, as if it were simply the possession of God's favourites. But in the Bible, the land is part of a bigger story than that, a story that warns against any sort of empty triumphalism.

Where do we come from? According to Genesis, we come from the decision of a God who shows endless, even alarming flexibility in arranging to stay near us, even when we show ourselves incapable of any stability in the place given us to occupy. We come from the Garden of Eden, the shortest golden age on record, where, before Adam and Eve have exchanged more than a sentence, they are caught up in the horribly recognisable fantasy of growing up and learning wisdom by magic not experience. We come from Noah's ark, where we have been stuffed into a small space in uncomfortable proximity to the rest of creation and made to face the fact that we are as vulnerable as any other inhabitant of this planet. We come from Ur of the Chaldees, a stable and secure enough place which doesn't have enough room for the dangerous presence of a free God, so that we have to uproot ourselves and find a place where we can hear something other than the soothing noises of a familiar society.

Alleluia for this odd family tree. Our family traditions, it seems, are rather unexpected ones, traditions of a style of human living that is marked by constant searching and new starts. It is a tradition of relying on the invisible companion who repeatedly upsets our attempts to domesticate him and to smooth out the problems of growing up as persons or as communities. Genesis is a story of how God's purposes are revealed and worked out; but it gives very little comfort to anyone who imagines that human access to these purposes is simple or even (most of the time) remotely accurate as to God's methods and timescales.

So that an alleluia for Genesis is a thanksgiving for what makes the Bible (in spite of rather a lot of misrepresentation by believers and unbelievers alike) so powerful an enemy of the way people talk about manifest destiny and God-sanctioned historical missions. The first real mission we know about in the Bible is Abraham's. He is called to two things: he has to be an ancestor for God's people and he is called away from what he thinks is home. He has to live from a future he can't see—which is very different from living out a script that's clear and achievable.

Biblical history reveals the God who, as the philosopher said, "writes straight with crooked lines." Genesis ends with the chosen people happily abandoning the Promised Land; yet we know in retrospect that somehow this will be integrated into one story. Later on, the people demand a king, against God's plainest advice; yet the kingship will become another sign of God's promise. King David is chosen by God; but his career, subject of the longest personal saga in the whole of the Bible, is a roller coaster of failure, flight, betrayal, danger, precarious recovery, tragic frustration, a story in which supernatural intervention is hardly ever around. In the complex human emotions and uncertainties of this drama, it is God's action that is going forward, and God's company that is the one secure constant.

We love the idea of destiny. As individuals and as nations, we walk so readily into the role of God's chosen agents, as we see it. Yet when God tells us about the life of his chosen agents in the Bible, it looks so different, so much more dangerous or simply so much more like ordinary human hard work. As so often, the Bible refuses to go along with our fantasies of guaranteed success. And at a time when religious rhetoric—from several quarters—about the mission to realise God's purpose in history is one of the things that most threatens the peace and sanity of the world, it should be a priority for Jews and Christians to witness to the Bible's firm commitment to the long perspective of God. "What would God do without me/us?" is a question that always lurks behind our enthusiasm for crusading of various kinds. It is the most deeply unbiblical question imaginable.

Humanity is all about "genesis," becoming; and the history of our religious growing up is all about becoming ourselves in the constant company of a God who is beyond all "genesis," beyond the processes of struggle and self-definition. Early Christians actually defined God as "the one who does not become" (and gave themselves a few intellectual headaches in the process). They were not complicating their thinking about God by messing around with Greek philosophy; they were just trying to be clear about why God was always there for people in the Bible story—because God was always free, never trapped in the circumstances of the "becoming" of his people. We can grow and change so radically just because God does not belong in our world of change.

Our relation to God is what provides the background against which change can still add up to a single story. For God's friends and God's people, the unity of our lives doesn't come from living out a great dramatic script but from the unseen, faithful presence of God alongside us in all our developing.

Genesis sets the tone for the whole of the Bible, and we do no justice at all to our Jewish and Christian Scriptures if we try to reduce them to stories of infallible discernment by impeccable heroes. What we read about is how God, having called us and shown us what kind of God it is that we have to do with, then adjusts to our misunderstanding and self-will, constantly refusing to let us be trapped forever in the fantasies and the prisons we invent for ourselves. In a very important sense, all of Genesis, and all of the rest of the Bible, is really a long explanatory note to the opening affirmation—that the God of this story is the one whose utterly free decision is what lies at the origin of everything. The beginning of all our stories, and the stories of the planets and protozoa and dinosaurs, is generosity. None of this needed to be; God wanted it so, out of the impulse of love. God wanted the divine life to be shared and echoed. God wanted to generate in time and change the sort of life that is his own—capable of love and freedom and relationship. What he just is, he repeats in the processes of becoming. And for that reason, when God engages with the history of human beings, we should know that what we shall meet is generosity and faithfulness.

So when we tell this story of our origins, we cannot use it to boost our pride or self-satisfaction, and we cannot use it to sanctify a particular passing state of affairs. All our worth and solidity comes from the delight that God takes in what he has made. The value of any thing or person is simply that by existing it expresses the joy of God. And we know that this or that passing state of affairs has value in the degree to which it spurs us on our way to that life which God intends, that full share in divine joy and liberty which is the goal of creation itself.

What we most fundamentally and truly are is what our relation to God makes us. When we explore our past, retrieve our memories, it should not be to search out some primitive truth about our isolated selves that will reveal our "real" selves, as individuals or as societies. It should be to enrich our wondering recognition of an active love that was there before we even existed, before the first verse of our own particular "genesis" story. Our alleluia for Genesis is in truth an alleluia for the silence that comes before Genesis, the pregnant, overwhelming silence of divine fullness preparing to create its own echo in the abundance of a created, changing world.

LIFE

Outside there are small fishing boats trolling the little island at the tip of the bay. On the hill above the sea, border collies are yapping at the heels of a quickening herd of sheep. Walkers are strolling along the Kerry Way, talking as they go, pausing every step or two to check another clump of early buds. And inside, on the television, Ireland is about to begin the Six Nations Rugby season by playing an Italian team on the Italian's home ground in Rome. You can almost feel the island begin to quiver from the excitement of it all.

I'm not fishing, I don't know a thing about sheep, I can't walk long distances, and I couldn't care less about rugby season. But I'm quivering, too. I'm alive, in the midst of all this, and there is an electricity to it that is as old as I am, as new as every dawn.

But life is more than a pastoral, however pastoral it may seem at any given moment.

To define life by its pastoral moments only—the goal of a feel-good society—is to understand very little about life at all. Life calls for stronger stuff than that. Life is dirge as well as symphony, lament as well as hymn.

The very notion of "life" is an unclear one in this day and age. It is no one thing for anyone—neither the rich nor the poor. It is many different things for different people and even for the same person at different times.

The questions life raises cry for resolution—and take a lifetime to answer. Is life good of its essence, or difficult by definition? Is it to be borne or, when we are beleaguered by the strain of it all, abandoned at will? Must we drink it to the dregs or can we surrender in the heat of the day?

The fact is that no matter how bucolic this moment here and now, it is not always so. Storms will capsize small boats. Sheep across the world will become diseased, herds will die, people will starve to death. The walkers will tire. The best of teams will lose. The fragility of life will make itself known again and again. At the wrong time. In the wrong place. To the wrong people.

While the boats in Ireland drifted in the sun, for instance, in my hometown across the sea an elderly woman of eighty-five has just been run over by an elderly man of eighty-four. Neither saw the other coming. Was her life over anyway? Does her death matter less because she had already lived so long? Is age a barrier to life? Does life leave us one day at a time? Or is it only time that goes, not life?

We wrestle with the questions of life without end. We wonder if there is really any such thing. And then we decide that there must be. Surely everything we see around us—all this energy, all this good, all this joy—has not been for nothing. Surely our lives have some kind of eternal meaning. Otherwise why the consciousness, why the pain?

There is always another way to look at life. There is always another side to everything.

Around the world people who had nothing to do with starting a war are dying in it. Whole peoples are underfed, overworked, underpaid, condemned to conditions they cannot change. So where is life in that? What of life is that? And what is there to be thankful for if all the dimensions of life are all so fragile, so fleeting? If love is temporary and not as lasting as we hope for, is it foolish to love? If growth and achievement are simply natural stages in every life, why work so hard to get them? If life is nothing but drudgery, why bother?

The truth is that all those elements—good and bad, painful as well as pleasant—are the alleluia points of life. Once love comes, alleluia becomes a descant of every day. Once we come to know our own abilities, we are able to give thanks for the gifts of others as well as our own. When we come to recognize that even drudgery can be joyful, can be fulfilling, there is nothing that can be asked of us that is too much to do if we want to do it. All these things are simply part of the process of living an alleluia life. And all of that living is what makes us who and what we are.

What's more, the vagaries of life give us all a chance over and over again to do today what we did not do last year or in another place or yesterday. Life, however interrupted, is one long moment of coming to be the best we can be. Life, we come to understand, is simply the process of growing into God.

But the growing is not linear. It is at best a process of stops and starts, of moments apparently without meaning and times that test the fiber of the soul.

Growing into God is not so much, then, the process of becoming perfect. Perfection is a human ideal, an arrogant one at that, but it is not a human state. Perfection is not ours to have.

On the contrary, to aspire to perfection is to doom ourselves to the kind of failure that can lead either to depression or to despair—neither of which is healthy, both of which only distract from the real purpose of life.

But consciousness is an entirely different thing. Consciousness makes the most mundane elements of life glorious. Consciousness tells us that there is nothing meaningless in life, that everything we do is bringing us closer and closer to where we're going, whether we know where that is or not. Then we surrender our notions of greatness or perfection and find that simply the process of allowing ourselves to become fully human is more than enough to make life worthwhile. We may be ants on a rock in space rather than giants astride the continents, yes, but, we come to realize, we are blessed ants, indeed.

Only when we recognize our own smallness can we possibly begin to cling to the greatness of God. It is often only at our low points in life—when the alcohol lays us flat on our faces in the dust, when the money runs out, when the other person gets the promotion—that we feel the Presence and hear the Voice within telling us that there is more in us than these things, that there is enough within us to make us happy without having to spend our lives grasping for empty straws. Then, secure in what we are rather than what we have, we suddenly know that there is nothing to fear. There is simply nothing outside of us that can possibly destroy the security within.

The problem is simply that it can take years to understand that. Every ad in every magazine is designed to tell us differently. We spend the years learning to track life, like a stalking horse on tour. Life is in good times, we think, a sign of our blessedness. Life is what we achieve, we're sure—all our titles, all our cars, all our children's diplomas. Life is some kind of public checklist—the good job, the condo on the beach, the big cars, the official invitations— which assures others that we are who we want them to think we are. They become signs of the shell of the self. They say merit, and competency, and worthiness, we think. We hope. But down deep we doubt it ourselves. Otherwise, why would we so much fear losing them? Without the big car, who am I? Without the corner office, what have I achieved? Without the house and the driveway, what have I done in life?

The problem is that life is not easily tracked. We travel with the right people and feel empty, nevertheless. We work hard all our lives and though, every once in a while, we get small glimpses of good times, the fortune never stays, the blessing is never secure. We keep all the social rules, but inner peace eludes us and the effort of them is always more routine than sweet.

Then the cataclysm comes, the moment we never wanted, never expected, never thought would happen. Then, there in the midst of the thing we wanted least or feared most, we find life raw and undiluted, erratic and uncontrolled. Then life comes in loss and leaves us to begin again. Life comes in surprises and requires us to adjust and grow. Life comes in the love of the one we never set out to find. Life comes in the very moments we expected least but live to the hilt. Life is in the surprising niches and crannies of life where we find ourselves face-to-face with the power of the universe and the resilience of our souls to deal with it.

Then life becomes creative possibility, not achievement. It beckons to us to become new again. It opens new doors and takes us down strange paths where we do not know the way but cannot not go. The death of those we love, the loss of what we want, the amazing apparition of joy we never before knew could even exist for us suddenly show us the underside, the other side, the exciting side of ourselves. And we grow in exciting new ways.

We begin to make distinctions then. Life is not one thing; it is at least three things.

Life is physical existence with all the limits and tasks that implies.

Life is emotional development with all the ecstasy and all the anguish that requires.

Life is the slow, steady cycle of spiritual growth, with all the many diversions we practice to avoid the real thing.

Life is not an alleluia for meeting the standards of an Avon ad or a business tycoon or a social maven. Life is the process of becoming emotionally, psychologically, and spiritually whole—mature, balanced, and lost in the consciousness that all these things I owe to the God who companions me through all the days of wandering to the core of it.

King David had to lose everything before he could possibly understand what life expected of him. Queen Esther, having finally risen to status, had to give it all up to be what she was meant to be in the world. They, and thousands like them whose lives veered from one pole to another along the way, show us that the alleluia for life is not a paean to the pastoral. It is the experience of having dealt with the surprises of life, opened our souls to things we never thought we wanted, and come to find that the essence of life is not in anybody's definition of perfection. Life is only in the search for it, in the acceptance of it in all its dimensions, at all its levels. It is in the consciousness that life is forever and always a work in progress. Every day. For all our years.

Then we come to know that life is only in the wholeness of it.

UNITY

In 1939 the German nation, all shouting "Heil Hitler" together, followed Adolph Hitler across Europe, raping nations of their independence, rampaging through villages and towns, suppressing foreign governments—intent on creating a Super Race and a Teutonic government in all of Europe. Germany was a country united in its quest for power, no matter what excuse was later designed to excuse it.

In 1960, John F. Kennedy was led to invade Cuba by a team of advisers who were all opposed to the Castro government, the one blatantly communist government in the heart of the Americas. Cuba was a small island country in the middle of the Caribbean, poor, underdeveloped, militarily weak. Together, the advisers, theorizing in an office in Washington DC, were certain of U.S. success. Unity for them was jingoism unchallenged. But the invasion failed, the United States was humiliated around the world, and the attack on the Bay of Pigs, meant to unseat Fidel Castro, only served to tighten his hold on the country.

In the sixteenth century, when Martin Luther challenged the practices of the Roman Catholic Church in its sale of indulgences, its hierarchical ordering of the spiritual life, and its suppression of the laity, the church in the Council of Trent closed ranks against the Reformers. For over four hundred years, as a result, the church castigated the Reformers, refused to see its own errors, refused to repent its heresies and arrogant misleading of the ignorant. Church became the ecclesiastical equivalent of pure and unadulterated political power. And it was all made possible because people refused to be self-critical, because they sold their souls and gave away their faith to the powers of the day.

Unity, it seems, can be a very dangerous thing.

On the other hand, the church in the Second Vatican Council united to question itself. Instead of assuming that its very time-bound statements were eternally true, it redefined its mission in a way that spoke to a modern age and, in the doing of it, recognized and reformed the specious theology Martin Luther had tried to warn it about four hundred years before.

The governments of Europe united to rebuild Germany after World War II and bring that great nation back to a point of pride and productivity, more intent than ever on creating a democratic society where people could think differently and stand together at the same time.

The United States, too, later risked the kind of unity that comes out of the hegemony of the powerful to integrate its black and white communities in what had been a quietly, but clearly, divided America.

Unity, it seems, is more than solidarity and more than uniformity. Unity, ironically, is a commitment to becoming one people who speak in a thousand voices. Rather than one message repeated by a thousand voices, unity is one message shaped by a thousand minds.

False unity is a not uncommon element, even today. Strong authority figures have two options. They may choose to lead by taking no suggestions, brooking no discussion, asking no questions of the population. These are those who control a group with answers. They may genuinely solicit and totally trust the wisdom of the group to replicate what has already been decided. But if they allow questions at all, they find them elsewhere. They question other groups but not their own. They question new questions but not the old answers. Indeed, their life is not built around questions; their life is built around answers that bind the group together in a common concern, a single optic.

And therein lies the difference between unity and uniformity. Unity is not external control; it is internal commitment derived one person at a time until what they hear from one another together touches the heart and drives the soul of them all.

Unity cannot be enforced; only uniformity can be imposed. But ideas that are imposed do not last long. They endure only as long as there is enough force behind them to require them. When the power to enforce a rule is lost, the group begins to splinter, to fragment, to lose its energy. Then people either leave the group or stay in it for other reasons: for the sake of tradition or social advantage or habit alone.

In times of great social change, as now, in times when the very foundations of life are in threat of collapsing, as now—when the very nature of life and death, of spirit and matter, of mind and body, of technology and people —are in question, the temptation is to avoid the ambiguities of the future by requiring the institutionalization of the past. Then churches tell people what they can think and governments tell people what they can't do, the courts make law and the military makes weapons. Then everything is made to look united again, but nothing really is.

Then we intuit what real unity is about and how to recognize it so that when the moment of its resurrection comes we may all sing a hearty alleluia on the mountaintop of our souls.

The kind of unity that is born out of differences and becomes the glue of a group has four characteristics: it frees, it enables, it supports, and it listens.

A group that is genuinely unified is a group that has freed every member to be themselves. In fact, the truly united group knows that every idea, every voice, counts in the process of idea formation. Without the collection of ideas, no consensus is possible. Then the group is reduced to the kind of compliance that wilts in the noon-day sun. Then we begin to hear: "Well, I never thought it was a good idea in the first place." Then we know that even at the height of its power, underneath it all the group lacked heart.

For the freedom to ask questions without reprisal in the face of contrary concepts, sing alleluia.

To seek unity means that enabling people to speak without fear and without hesitation must become the cornerstone of discussion. Ideas must be sought out. Answers must be elicited. Hesitations must be defined. Cautions must be honored before unity in diversity is possible. But when it comes, sing alleluia because then all the talents of the population are wholeheartedly engaged in the enterprise.

For a people to know unity they must also know the support that comes when people who speak another truth are as respected for that perception as they would have been for agreeing with the majority in the first place. I can only give myself to a group that not only tolerates my differences but seeks them out. That way, when a decision is finally forged out of the fire of differences, there is no doubt that it carries within it all the passion the group has to give.

Finally, unity depends on listening, not only to begin it but also to sustain it. No decisions are made once and forever. No unity can be perpetual if it revolves around a changing center. No good thing can be guaranteed to stay good throughout time. It is so easy to make an idol out of a time, a place, a decision, a group that once was united but now, in the light of another, newer day, is not.

Then it is time to begin again. Then the unity must be tested and reshaped. It is a very holy process, the search for unity. It is an alleluia moment made for eternity but welded and rewelded by time.

The unity of the church to which we look back with such nostalgia never existed cemented in time as we like to fantasize it. The unity of the state was never more clear than when the founders hammered out ideals that confronted every known assumption and honored the existence of every human being.

The unity existed when Paul confronted Peter and Peter recognized the truth of the unity called for in the

Jewish-Gentile community. Unity was the hallmark of the first Council of Jerusalem and the first Constitutional Convention, where no agendas were declared off-limits and no concerns were smothered.

Out of the tension of opposites in each came a unity that forged a church and a nation and gave them the flexibility to continue over time. For that sing alleluia.

OTHERNESS

The barrage of political hype that deluged us before we left for Russia charged the trip with a kind of random electricity. Russia—still "the Soviet Union"—the subtexts said clearly, was a feared and fearsome place. What's more, any kind of benign interpretation of that concern would be at our own peril. They had all warned us. They had all tried to save us. They had all tried to prepare us for the worst. The only question was whether or not we would be smart enough to listen. The messages of fear came from all sides.

In the first place, we had been praying for years—after every Mass, in fact—for "the conversion of Russia." The substance of the church's language had been clear enough: Here was a country that intended to swallow us all up and make us atheists.

In the second place, if the subliminal messages from the church weren't bad enough, the messages from the state were even worse.

I had traveled before, but not like this. To cement our caution we got bulletins from the State Department almost weekly, and travel warnings from the embassy in every packet of preparatory material and a myriad of personal anecdotes from government spokespeople about being secretly bugged and secretly followed and falsely arrested. Under no conditions should we stray away from the group. Under no conditions should we meet with private groups. Under no conditions should we change money through the underground money changers who operated in clear sight on the main streets of Moscow. If we got into trouble, whatever that was, there was nothing they could do for us.

This was no tourist excursion, the messages implied; this was the Real Thing, the Big Time, the Cloak and Dagger game writ large. And we were in it and they were all around us: Russians. The KGB. A strange, dour, rancid people to whom life meant nothing and ours even less. And all for no reason whatsoever. Forget the nuclear bomb. Forget the fact that Russia had been invaded nine times in its history, all of them after signing peace treaties with Western powers. Forget anything other than that this was a nefarious, godless, and bearish people who would eat us all alive if they could.

I went to Russia with an open heart but looking over my shoulder at every street corner. No one and nothing came near to the bogeymen I expected.

Russian hosts presented hand-drawn copper hangings off their living room walls as a personal gift because, to make polite conversation, I had simply said that I liked them.

A man in the metro station who realized that we needed directions but could not himself speak enough English to make them clear to us crossed Moscow on the subway with us and, having deposited us at the station we were seeking, got into another train and went back to where he had begun.

A group of women laborers in a tractor plant, dressed in cotton smocks and headscarves, surrounded me. "Peace, please; peace, please," they said with tears in their eyes. "Tell your American people, 'Peace, please.'"

The congregation in a Russian Orthodox church pressed forward to hear the priest introduce our group as peacemakers from the United States—and then lifted me by my elbows above the happy, clapping crowd to carry me off the altar at the end of my very simple little comments about them, about us, about peace between us.

Villagers laid out long, rough-cut tables covered with peasant food while the musicians played and danced around us.

Every day, every place we went, simple Soviet people contradicted the image of wild, ungodly, and uncontrollable human beings of whom we needed to be afraid.

These were the Russians. These were the "other." These were people. Just like us.

For the first time in my life I began to understand the philosophical concept of "otherness," the heresy that says that we, of all the world, are unique: Uniquely good, uniquely righteous, uniquely generous, uniquely kind, uniquely human.

But with the diminishment of the concept of the malicious, inferior, unreasonable other went the justification for war, the authorization for prejudice, the warrant for stereotyping, and the mandate for burning the unknown other at the stake. "Who would we not love," Mary Lou Kownacki writes, "if we only knew their story?"

Russia, we have decided, is no longer our enemy. We have uncocked our missiles and torn up our propaganda pieces and turned our sites on other "others." Now more likely targets. Now more sustainable enemies. Now more politically advantageous opponents. Now we find "other" in men, in women, in gays, in Arabs, in liberals, in conservatives.

We look for differences and call them "bad" rather than simply "different."

But "otherness" is an alleluia gift of great measure that takes us out of ourselves, beyond ourselves, into the best of ourselves.

Being open to the "other" expands our vision of the world. The world is not simply us. It is a profusion of differences in concert. We do not sing all the parts. We are not the stars of the show. We are simply part of the cast of extras called humanity.

When we open ourselves to "otherness," we open ourselves to learning. We come to know that there are other ways to go about things, as well as other people unlike us. We find out that there is no single way to do anything. There is no perfectly right way and there are few absolutely wrong ways. There are only "other" ways. Just as effective. Just as intelligent. Just as good. Simply other.

To become immersed in "otherness" may be, in the end, the only way we ever really come to understand what humanity really is. It is black and yellow, red and brown. And on the side, it is a little white, beginning now to blend everywhere into something else.

"Otherness" is what calls us to be more than our ghetto selves. And that is reason for alleluia like no other.

When Jeremiah saw the vision of the presence of God suspended over Babylon as well as over Jerusalem, he realized that he had to give up everything he had ever thought about Israel, about God, about the world. Until that moment, a Jerusalemite, he had been convinced that YHWH shone about Jerusalem alone and for Jews only. But now, seeing the presence of God poised protectively over Babylon—today's Iraq—he also realized that what he got instead was a God who was greater, a people that was broader, and a world that was holier than he had ever imagined.

It is the God of the "others" whom we too seldom come to know, and so we remain spiritual orphans whose God is too often only ourselves speaking—and at full volume.

Who is the "other"? The "other" is anyone who is not made in our image and likeness. It is anyone who is not ourselves. It is the one who is not of our race or our faith tradition or our citizenry or our language. It is the one who shows us to ourselves.

The "other" is the one who teaches us that we are not the whole world. We are only a piece of it waiting for the "Other" to make us more than we were when we began. Alleluia.

Past

Travis is a tall, handsome boy who came from a family of five children from three fathers and a mother with a couple of live-in boyfriends on the side. The mother worked hard all their lives to function half awake–half asleep on lithium. The sister married young and left town; the other boys drifted; Travis worked from odd job to odd job from the time he was eight years old, saving his money, buying the clothes no one could give him. He liked to draw houses when he was a little boy and talked about being an architect. In the end he joined the Marines to get the education he couldn't otherwise afford. He won't be back to this neighborhood any more. Travis was a poster child for a neighborhood built on dreams.

The part of town I live in isn't . . . well, let's just say it isn't posh. It's simple and old and pretty well kept up, given the circumstances. But it's unfashionable. That's a word that means that nobody I know wants to live there.

It isn't simply that the neighborhood lacks style. No, it's far worse than that. My neighborhood lacks couth. People on this block are not suave or finespun or refined. Where I live, they live life close to the bone. They work two jobs or they don't work at all. They keep life together, but barely, and always at great cost to themselves. Their money doesn't make money while they sleep because they don't have any extra money to put away at night. The money they have, they spend every day on food and rent and diapers.

It's always been that way, in fact. Every group that has ever moved into this part of town has simply stayed there long enough to be able to afford to move out. First the Germans came and left, then the Polish, then the blacks, then the Hispanics, then the Russians. Now Asians from a wide swath of the world are the people in waiting here. These people did not come over on the Mayflower. They are not prone to magnify their origins. They spend their lives trying to outlive them, in fact.

In this neighborhood, those with a penchant for education creep their way out of the center of town one block at a time. Those for whom education has never really been an asset simply sink to the bottom and have another generation of children for whom, they hope, life will eventually get better.

My neighborhood is one of those places people remember when they talk about their "past." And most of them don't. On the contrary. Most of them struggle one job at a time to get to the suburbs and then spend the rest of their lives trying to forget where they've come from.

That's what's so strange about the past. That's what's so interesting about the past. The fact is that the past is never really past. We live with it every minute of every day of our lives. As the philosopher Henri Bergson put it: "The present contains nothing more than the past, and what is found in the effect was already in the cause." We live our past every day of our lives. Wherever we are, we are the product of what we've come from. We spend time trying to undo and redo and do over what we know ourselves, down deep, to really be.

The past colors the way we look at today and think about tomorrow. It forms our very definition of ourselves.

The past never, ever really leaves any of us. All of us come from something—an alcoholic home, incest, embarrassing poverty, perhaps. That's why it is so important, both to our spiritual life and to our psychological well-being, that we come to be able to sing our alleluias about it.

The fact of the matter is that though we can change where we live, we can't change how we were formed. However difficult, however "unnatural" Travis's upbringing may seem to some people, it served him well. Those who take for granted a marriage and family life that provides a kind of nest in which everyone in the group is nurtured and protected within the home may wince at the thought of little boys on their own so much, but Travis's past has nurtured some very strong qualities in him. He was formed to take care of himself. And he does. He has an inner strength and self-reliance unusual for his age. He has survived being alone and so knows that aloneness will never destroy him now.

Deep inside all of us is a Travis who learned something from the past that marks him yet today. Whatever those learnings, they make us strong in the present and capable of facing an unknown future. Whatever we endured taught us endurance. Whatever we wanted taught us to pursue a goal. Whatever we learned to do without taught us that we will always be capable of doing without, an important quality for the lean times.

The past stores up inside us a veritable gallery of models from which we draw life patterns yet.

I remember from my own past the woman down the hall with diabetes who lay in her bed day after day, legs long gone, but smiling as she crocheted blankets for the rest of the family. She stays in my heart, reminder of the fact that it is possible to suffer the worst and never sour under it.

I remember the deaf young man down the street who taught me sign language because he had no one to talk to, and whose sign language alphabet card I keep in my Bible yet to remind me that no one comes into your life unless you reach out to them.

I remember the gruff old man who sat on a stool in the alley swearing at children as they walked wide circles around him and from whom they all learned to swear back.

They walk with me, these ghosts from the past, smiling at me, signing to me, warning me that it is possible to isolate myself in a small, mean world and to take others with me there if I want to live a world unto myself.

Indeed, the past is a storehouse of the memories that have formed us and shaped us and prepared us for worlds far beyond the one in which we grew.

But the past is even more than its treasury of the yesterdays that marked us with their sadnesses and deprivations and struggles and lingering flashes of the first meanings of love. The past is all we know of the possibilities we each harbor within us. The past burns into our flesh, like a flaming brand, the awareness that what we have survived before, bested before, done before, we can do again.

The best proof we have against destruction and despair is our memories of having wrestled with life before now—and prevailed. These are what sustain the young woman, a long-ago incest victim, who begins to recognize as part of her healing that, whatever the trauma she's been through, she is, after all, a survivor. These are what go with the man who withstood taunts about his thick glasses from the other children in school to become the class valedictorian years later, who knows that he has been freed of any allegiance to the emotional control of others. These are the mainstay of the young widow who was raised by her widowed mother and knows that she can do it, too, and that her children will be no worse developed by the specter of the broken family because she herself is not.

Why bother to remember the past? Because the past is the one proof we have that the present is possible. "Many are always praising the bygone time," Caleb Bingham wrote, "for it is natural that the old should extol the days of their youth; the weak, the time of their strength; the sick, the season of their vigor; and the disappointed, the spring-tide of their hopes."

In the final analysis, then, the past is an alleluia for graces then unknown and now full of meaning. "Even though you intended to do harm to me," Joseph says to the brothers who, out of rivalry for their father's love, sold him into slavery in Egypt, "God intended it for good, in order to preserve a numerous people, as he is doing today. So have no fear; I myself will provide for you and your little ones."

Every moment of life is an alleluia moment for the past. One of the major graces of life is to come to realize that.

Peace

I can see all of them yet as if it were yesterday. Three old images crowd my mind and confuse my thoughts and confound my soul when I try to explain what it means to talk about peace, to be grateful for peace, to become peaceful.

The first is the sight of American soldiers advancing onto the campus of Kent State University and firing automatic weapons into crowds of students who were staging a loud but peaceful protest against the draft during the Vietnam War.

The second is the sight of another group of students sitting huddled together for strength in Tiananmen Square in the heart of Beijing. Singing, chanting slogans, refusing to move, they were implacable in their petition for social and economic change. Day after day thousands sat there at the seat of government, defying the government to dare to slaughter so large a crowd of unarmed young people and intellectual leaders in the name of "keeping order."

The third image in my mind is the memory of one lone Chinese boy who, rising from the midst of the protesters in Tiananmen Square, stood in front of a moving tank whose orders were to sweep the square empty of anyone who dared to remain there once ordered to leave. The boy stood, head bowed, shoulders straight, feet planted squarely on the pavement. It was one unarmed boy against a Chinese tank. Suddenly, the tank stopped moving.

The pictures were chilling ones, beamed around the world to every nation on earth, all of whom had their own internal oppressions, their own powerless majorities with which to deal.

The scenes, different as they were in culture and content, begged a million questions, but all of them, ultimately, had only one underlying theme:

What was the power of power in the face of peaceful resistance?

In the United States the scene of the shootings at Kent State shocked the nation. Almost immediately the tenor of the country began to change. Its support of the war began to erode. Its willingness to force-feed its children to the yawning mouth of the war machine ended.

In China a nation began to get a glimpse of its own invincible ability to confront power with power—if it ever wanted to make the forces clear. After all, it may mean certain death to go into conflict without a weapon. But, on the other hand, no amount of weapons guarantees survival when we are all using them.

The power of the spirit had never been more clear than in the face-off between the tank and the thin young man. All the power in the world could not make the boy move, could not destroy his strength of spirit, could not break his resolve. Nor could it move the driver of the tank to an act of public barbarism in the name of public order.

"Peace hath her victories," Milton wrote, "no less renowned than war." All the weapons in the world, in other words, were, in the end, for nothing.

Peace is such a powerful presence.

The ancients tell the story of a warlord the tales of whose cruelty preceded him from village to village. People were terrified by his tortures and his murderous glee. Everywhere he went, he found the villages long evacuated before his triumphant coming.

At the last village he entered, the cooking pots still belched steam, the coals still burned, the tables were still set just as they had been when word of his coming reached the fleeing villagers. "I can see," the warlord smirked to his aide, "that all the people have already gone." His aide paused a moment. "Well, sir," he said. "Not quite all. One old monastic refuses to go."

The warlord howled in rage. "Bring that one to me immediately," he bellowed.

When they dragged the old monastic before the commander, the general roared for all to hear, "Do you not know who I am? I am he who can run you through with a sword and never even bat an eye."

And the old monastic looked up at the warlord calmly and replied, "And do you not know who I am? I am the one who can let you run me through with a sword—and never even bat an eye."

A commitment to peace, to being peaceful, to peacefulness draws from a very deep well. It is a source beyond the corruptions of either ambition or pride. It transcends addiction to either power or personality cults.

Ambition wilts in the face of peacefulness. The peaceful person knows the grace of being content with who he or she is. No titles or tenure are needed to assure such a one of her or his worth; therefore no one and nothing can threaten it. The serenity and satisfaction we feel on the inside cannot possibly be bested by anything outside ourselves. Therefore there is no reason to grasp and claw for it.

Pride, too, the need to supersede another person, to draw more attention, to consume more of the light in the room than the others do, to remind the world constantly of our superiority fades in the face of peacefulness. The only turf I seek is the space to be myself and so to be comfortable with life.

Once peace comes to a person, the need for power simply disappears and goes to dust inside ourselves. We are enough for us. There is no reason to suppress the other, no need to make sure that no head in the room is higher than our own.

All the need for wars, either public or personal, evaporates. There is nothing valuable enough to gain from them to risk either the loss of the peace or the death of the other.

So we say an alleluia for the coming of peace, for the death of ambition, for the passing of pride that enables us to be happy with who we are and what we have.

And how does peace come? Simple. By accepting who we are and what we have as enough for us. By recognizing and respecting who the other is and what they have as theirs. By finding within ourselves "the pearl of great price," the richest thing there is in life, the sense of the presence of the God who loves and companions us through all the pressures of life. "In moderating, not in satisfying, desires," Reginald Heber wrote, "lies peace."

Then we find that we have changed. We have become peaceful. We have come to realize now that we have all we need. We begin to see that our own role in life is only to spread the peace we have.

Then we begin to dedicate ourselves to that highest possible level of humanity that not only does good but, most of all, does no harm. We come to understand that simply doing good can be such a political ploy. Election periods abound in promises to do good that are no more than some kind of social bribe. To do no harm, on the other hand, requires real care, genuine compassion, true realization that the glow of the other diminishes no glow of my own. Then my own life begins to shine even more.

When Jacob puts all his wealth, all his household, all his herds, and all himself at the service of his brother Esau whom he had wronged, peace comes. But by this time Esau, too, has changed, has put down pride and ambition, greed and the need for power, and has no need of those things whatsoever. Alleluia.

SUFFERING

The story is a charming one. It also smacks of the pathetic. It brings us to confront within ourselves two separate kinds of suffering.

The first comes from circumstances beyond our control. The house burns down, for instance. Or the company moves the corporation and the job I loved goes with it. Or the savings we thought would always be there get eaten up in medical bills. Whatever the nature of the trauma, we find ourselves in situations in which we can do nothing but live through, endure, survive. But at least we do not blame ourselves for them.

In this kind of suffering something is taken from us that we always knew could disappear—but never really thought would disappear. The house has always been in our family. The company has been there forever. I'm not reckless about money.

This kind of suffering changes our lives, perhaps, but it does not eat us alive from the inside out, full of anger, full of self-blame.

The second kind of suffering, however, comes from things we do to ourselves, things of our own making that plague us for years. These are the sufferings that tear us apart inside.

This story of suffering hinges on a bit of both.

Ishaq Levin and Zebulon Simentov, the papers reported, were the last two Jews in Afghanistan. Afghanistan's Jewish community had once numbered as many as forty thousand Jews after, the reports say, "Persian Jews fled forced conversion in neighboring Iran." But the figures declined over the years. After the creation of the state of Israel in 1948, most of the remaining Jews emigrated there, the rest of them after the Soviet invasion of 1979.

Finally only Ishaq and Zebulon were left to live under the repressive rule of the Taliban, dwelling at opposite ends of the synagogue, mortal enemies who never spoke to one another. Instead, they blamed one another for everything: for the way the Taliban treated them, even for the surrender of the last Torah to the regime.

It was a miserable time, outside and in. Rather than live in mutual support of one another in so harrowing a system, they lived in mutual distrust.

Finally, a few months before the invasion of Afghanistan by the United States, worried about his imminent death, Levin said he "begged Simentov not to be his enemy." He worried, he said, that if the enmity continued there would be no one who could bury him in the traditions of his religion.

Ishaq Levin died in January 2005 at the age of eighty. Simentov was forty-five, now the only Jew left in Afghanistan. No one from whom to learn the tradition; no one to whom to pass it on.

In the end, Simentov's family in Israel passed on the news of Ishaq's death to the Levin family in Israel, and as a result, ironically, Levin had the largest state burial on the Mount of Olives in Jerusalem that a Jew can have.

Pathetic. On both counts. A pathetic way to live. A pathetic way to die—unknown and unloved.

Nevertheless, the story cries out to the rest of us to stop and consider how we ourselves deal with the sufferings we cause for ourselves and what there is in them that demands from us an alleluia for the hard times.

Clearly, suffering calls us to conversion, to that change of attitude that softens our hearts to one another and opens our arms to life in all its shapes and forms. In the gardens of Derrynane House on the Iveraigh Peninsula of Ireland a great old tree, once a towering master of the forest, lies parched, grey, and uprooted across an opening in the glade, its branches bare and stick-like. But the strange thing is that across the top of the old Goliath new growth of moss and ground pine has taken strong root. This tree is, for all practical purposes, living again, but in ways far different than was ever expected. The conversion from one kind of tree to another is the very icon of what it means to be converted of heart, to be different after we have died to one thing and in the process become another, just as strong and just as beautiful, however different now.

But suffering is not only a gift to the sufferer. Suffering is what enables us to understand the other as well. It is the ground of compassion. How is it that people are able to suffer and not feel for the suffering of the other? When we become part of that small population who are isolated from the joy of the rest of the world by pain, we alone are able to speak the language of grief that the other needs to hear.

It is easy to tell the other that we are "sorry for their troubles," as the Irish say, but until there is an edge of our own in the saying of it, the words never ring true.

The psalmist is quite clear about the situation: "In my good days," Psalm 20 says, "I thought I would never be disturbed." Until we ourselves have borne the blows of life it is so easy to become swaddled in the superficial. Suffering is what puts us in touch with the rest of the human race.

But suffering is not a steady-state position. On the contrary. It is suffering that moves us to rethink life, to find other kinds of meaning in life, to realize that life is made up of stages, each different from the last, each one a new challenge—and a new pitfall—as we begin to negotiate the tasks peculiar to each of them.

We begin to ask a new questions of life as we deal with suffering. We consider everything we're doing and wonder, "Is this worth it?" Is this worth my time in a life that gets increasingly shorter? Is it worth my energy, my effort? Is it worth what I cannot do while I'm doing this instead?

The question leads us to focus on worthier things than status or property or social contacts. It leads us to focus on our own ongoing growth and wisdom.

Suffering, we learn from Ishaq Levin, skills us in the process of "putting things down." It is one thing to live in Afghanistan under the Taliban. It is another thing to ourselves be the Taliban of our oppression. The grudges that choke the air out of our souls, the resentments that build up barriers, the petty competitions, the hurts so old we can't even remember now where or when they began all come to look different in the face of death. They look small. They look tawdry. They look useless. They look embarrassing. Have we really spent our lives on such things as these?

When we have suffered enough not to care if the hurts of life have all been healed but only that they no longer bind us, we have finally learned to live. What could be more worth an alleluia than that?

Second Kings 7 gives us a stark model of the prison into which our self-made sufferings cast us. Four lepers sit at the city gate, victims of the Aramean siege of Samaria. It has been a bleak and bitter time. The city is starving and demoralized. The nobles are eating the bony heads of donkeys; the poor are eating their own children. The situation is dire and the lepers know it.

"If we go out to the camp of the enemy, and they do not accept us," they reason, "they may well kill us. But if we stay in this place where we are, we will surely die."

So they leave the gates of their city and venture out into the dark, over the hills to a camp and a people, a place and a situation that are totally foreign to them. But, scripture tells us, by the time they get there the Arameans, thinking they are being pursued by a hired band of mercenaries, have left the camp, treasure in place and tables set. Suddenly free of the specter of death and flush with rich foods in a starving world, the lepers find themselves free, liberated, on the verge of a totally new life.

Alleluia for the sufferings that move us beyond our smaller, less-developed selves.

CRISES

In Colorado, a young mountain climber went out to do what he did best and loved most. He was, in fact, a noted outdoorsman, a professional survivalist despite his youth. But on this day the boy who had never faced anything catastrophic in his life, had never experienced anything about the outdoors he could not handle, slipped on the face of the rock wall to which he clung and found himself caught between shifting boulders. One arm was free, but the other lay locked between masses of granite that weighed tons. Three days later rescue teams had still not found him. Now time had become as much an enemy as a friend, as much a danger as the great rock ravine itself.

Desperation nibbled at the back of his mind. If he couldn't somehow free himself and walk out of this place, thirst and hunger would find him before the search party did. He might never get out of the crevasse into which he had fallen. It was his last chance and he knew it.

So he did the only thing he could to change his situation. He broke his wrist with a stone, amputated his trapped hand with his pocket knife and then, weak from hunger and loss of blood, walked back out of the canyon the very way he had walked into the place days before.

Months later, with a prosthesis on his hand and special rock climbing gear on his back, the young man returned to the canyon and climbed the same cliff, this time with one hand.

Perhaps the most interesting part of the story is that he did not go back to the place, the climb, the danger to make some kind of macho statement about his strength or bravado. He went back to where he almost died to celebrate his gratitude for life.

I watched the video of the climb with the kind of awe a person reserves for the unbelievable.

At first glance, I thought, it seems to be an unusual story. Then I realized how wrong that analysis really was. Crisis is not unusual for any of us. On the contrary. Though this situation is a particularly dramatic one, the fact of the matter is that it is far more ordinary than we are likely to think. Everyone falls into a crevasse someplace along the way in life. And, like the young climber fighting for his life, everyone has to amputate something to survive it.

In the end, it is not the fall that matters. It is having to give up some part of the self to survive the fall that is the most difficult part. But crisis always demands a price. That is the nature of crisis.

Crisis happens when the ordinary turns deadly on us, veers off the road, lands us upside down on the path we had long taken for granted and cuts us off from the predictable, the regular, the expected, the ordinary part of life. Crisis is what surprises us in the noontime of our lives and leaves us in blinding invisibility. No one knows we're reeling from the fall. No one comes to help. There is, between us and collapse, only ourselves.

Sometimes crisis comes in the form of financial loss—investments gone wrong, bills we never expected—that change a lifestyle or a sense of security. Sometimes it comes in terms of public reputation—the corners we cut at tax time or the relationship we never meant to have—that compromise the public face of things. Sometimes it comes in the form of the divorce or the job loss we never saw coming but that now leaves us with no place to call home, no one to call dear, nothing to call success.

Then we are left in the wilderness of the intransigent, facing emotional death, and desperate to find a way out of it all. All of life has changed and left us wanting.

Where is God now? Where is God here? How can anyone possibly find anything here to which they can honestly sing an alleluia?

But there are, in fact, great alleluia moments to be celebrated in a time of crisis, and they are different from the alleluias we discover in times of darkness or suffering.

Darkness is a time of confusion. We find ourselves waiting for clarity, for direction.

Suffering is a time of endurance. It tests our capacity simply to bear what is not changeable.

Crisis, however, marks the eruption points in life. It is the junction of the ordinary and the cataclysmic, the place in life where change comes with a vengeance.

Crisis, then, is a test of the deepest parts of the self. It measures what there is in us that is truly full of life. It ferrets out in us the part of us that, however much we wish could die, simply refuses to die. It is a very wholesome moment, this choice for life in the face of death.

Crisis is not about clarifying the moment or enduring the moment. Crisis requires resolution. It is about action. It is about negotiating the turning points in the road.

The alleluia moment in crisis comes when we finally realize that life is not about one thing, it is about many things. It is about parts of ourselves that we have not recognized yet, yes, but it is also about parts of the self that are meant to go if we are ever to live life in ways we never thought possible.

As a result of crisis we come to understand that there is no one single way that a life must be shaped if I am to be happy. In fact, happiness comes when I am finally doing what I was meant to do in the first place. Sometimes only when that bough breaks under us are we ever free to leave the relationship, leave the job, leave the public role and simply start over again. Differently. "Crises refine life, " Allan K. Chalmers writes. "In them you discover what you are."

Crisis confronts us with a reservoir of new strength, those parts of us that never had to be tested before—the person who doesn't have to do the expected and the predictable: marry the sorority girl, work in the family bank, own the gated condo. But crisis also changes our entire life. Things that seemed like second nature to us we have to put down now, amputate from our psyches, divorce from our expectations. It is a moment of new life.

There are those, of course, who buckle in a time of crisis. There are others who simply strike off in different directions with all the same talents and find life beyond the boundaries of their previous selves, more self than ever. There are some who buckle first and then touch in themselves the will to live again—and are now freer than ever to begin. "As we wake or sleep, we grow strong or we grow weak," Bishop Westcott said, "and at last some crisis shows us what we have become."

David faces Goliath and becomes the Goliath within him. We must all sing alleluia for the opportunity to do the same.

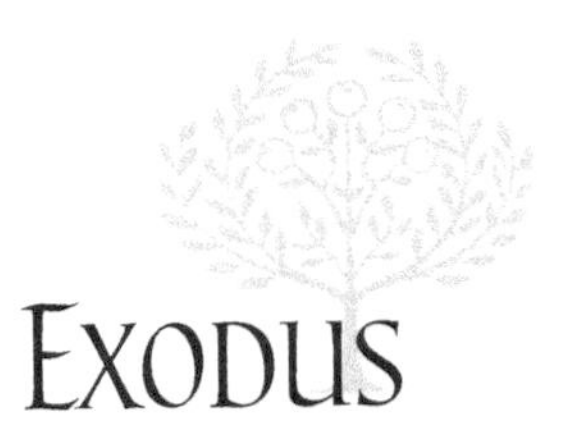

Exodus

If Genesis shows us what kind of God we have to do with, Exodus spells this out in a very particular bit of history, the history that made God's people not just an ethnic unit but a community that becomes distinctive because of the balance and equity of its relationships. Exodus is a story of slaves being set free, but it is also, crucially, a story about what happens when people try to come to terms with their freedom. And one of the things it tells us, as commentators have noticed from very early on, is just how reluctant people are to accept freedom when it is given them. In the story of Exodus, Moses has to battle not only against the king of Egypt but against his own fellow Israelites. They are suspicious of him when he first appears; they blame him when their conditions are made worse by a vindictive system reacting to the threat to its security. When they have actually left Egypt, there is nostalgia for lost comforts. They don't want to trust the alarming, invisible God who has dragged them away from their familiar ways, and they try to substitute an idol.

It's often said that the best tool of the oppressor is the mind of the oppressed. If you can convince someone that their subjection is not only normal but in everyone's real interests, you are likely to be very safe. And throughout history both slaves and slave owners have been ready to assume that the master-slave relationship is the default position for human beings. One set of people naturally and normally take responsibility for defining what another set can do, think, say, even what they are able to think and say about themselves. Breaking through this needs a powerfully clear sense that no earthly power has the right to define what any group of human beings can be or think, because—as we saw in thinking about Genesis—only God can do this.

But wait a moment. Isn't this just removing the problem one stage up the line? If human beings can't be told who they are by others, why exactly is it any better to be told who they are by God than to be told it by other people? What's good news about being released from human slavery only to be recaptured by another sort of slavery? Broadly speaking, this has been the way in which Western modernity has read the story told by Jews and Christians. Obedience to God is another kind of imposition. Real liberation will only come when God too is dethroned.

There is a certain plausibility to this—but only if we have forgotten exactly what kind of God it was that we met in Genesis. This God is not another individual pursuing a private agenda, defending his interests. He is the life that animates everything. The real exodus story begins when he says to Moses from the burning bush, "I am who I am." He doesn't need to negotiate, defend, argue, control. So when we say that only in relation to him can we become ourselves, we are not ascribing to God the "liberties" of a tyrant. It's more like saying, "If you want to swim, you must begin to understand the sea." This is the element in which you move. The nature of the love that makes and sustains us naturally shapes our possibilities; if we won't follow the rhythm of the divine ocean, we shan't learn to swim; we shall be struggling against the very life, the very conditions, that are upholding us. Real sin is actually hard work, requiring a huge capacity to go against the grain (which is why, as I was suggesting earlier, Augustine was right in saying that most sin carried with it a sense of miserable failure and frustration).

Real freedom is the freedom of the swimmer in the water or the performer caught up in the music—a freedom to find strength and joy in responding to the rhythm of what's actually there. So when God sets his people free, it isn't for some vague paradise of endless consumer choice, but for that kind of response to reality. Truth will make us free, says Jesus in the Fourth Gospel, because then we are stripped of all those fantasies about ourselves and the world that blind us to what we can and can't do (remember what was said in an earlier chapter about sin as plain illusion, like some obsessive convinced that they can make the world run by different rules). And this makes sense of the way Exodus is structured. The great event of liberation is followed by a stark and demanding period in which the freed slaves have to get used to a new climate, a new landscape. And as they do, they are confronted with responsibility: not only can they and must they become answerable for who they are—they also have to answer for each other.

This is what the giving of the law is all about. "Freedom means responsibility"—when we hear that sort of thing, it sounds rather depressing, as though freedom had to be restrained in some way. But the giving of the law in Exodus isn't an emergency measure to stop the Israelites getting out of hand. It's what their freedom is for. Now at last they can be what God has made them to be; they can be creative. They can craft together a way of living; they can shape each other's lives not by the impositions of slavery but by making the conditions in which others can have the same liberty. Exodus charts an extraordinary story of growing to maturity. At first, the freed slaves are like the maddening children in the back of the car: "Are we nearly there?" "Isn't there anything nicer to eat?" "Why can't we go home now?" And God treats them as capable of becoming real adults, who can take responsibility for one another. He gives the law so that each and every one of them will be able to depend on each and every other for their security and flourishing, without anxiety and fear.

Justice, in the Jewish Scriptures, is something a lot more interesting than what we often mean by the word. We tend to reduce it to "fairness," to people's ability to get what's due to them. But in the biblical context, it's about a whole climate of social health, about the kind of life together that both rests on and reinforces trust. "Doing justice," in the language of the Bible, is more than giving people their rights; it is living and acting in such a way that God's passionate care for and involvement in each person's welfare becomes visible. Law is a sort of sacrament, an active sign of who and what God is. Which is why, in Jewish Scripture, especially the Psalms, we are encouraged to give thanks for the law—not because we have been given horrible warnings about the results of going wrong (though that is not to be ignored), but much more because we have the opportunity to live in the most meaningful way possible: our decisions and policies and relationships can speak of God.

The human being envisaged by Exodus is someone who has begun to see that being in God's company as a free person gives her the capacity to set others free for the same creative service. Instead of living in an uneasy truce between competing interests, this person knows that what is most real and life-giving for all of us is a life in which we are mutually nourishing our joy and our responsibility, our ability to relate to God and each other sanely. The Ten Commandments are not an afterthought in this picture but an integral picture of what freedom looks like. Understandably, they begin by making us think about our relation to God. Don't let anything get between you and the living God; don't try to substitute for the living God the objects and images you think you can comfortably cope with or control; don't try to use God for your own purposes, as if he had given you magic words to manipulate the world. Be sure that each week you spend time with God that is free from the pressure of business, problem-solving, or acquisition. And then we are told to turn to our fellow humans. What is due to those who gave us life? Be grateful and let it show. What is due to others who seek the same liberty as ourselves? Never imagine that anyone is dispensable. Keep the promises you have made and honour the promises of others in the world of human relations. Remember that the security you seek is what all want, and don't set out to invade. Tell the truth about yourself and others. Don't imagine that what makes someone else secure and happy is exactly what you need to make you secure and happy if only you could get it from them.

A mature human society would be one that looked like this, so Exodus claims. This is what responsibility amounts to. It is a deep concern not to lose sight of the radical otherness of God and an equally deep concern that we should both recognise what everyone desires and see the need for respect towards each other as each discovers this in diverse ways. We are in one sense looking for the same thing. But what saves this from competitive anxiety is the constructive pattern of lives interweaving and serving one another.

We have done some very odd things to the idea of freedom in the last couple of hundred years. We have identified it with the right to accumulate unlimited possessions; with the right to unrestricted pleasure and gratification; with the maximum level of individual choice in everything from automobiles to health care to sexual partners. In such a cultural environment, the Exodus vision ought to give us something of a jolt. It says that there are some things about human beings that are not negotiable, simply because they are engaged in conversation with God quite independently of any other relationships, and their lives are (swimmers in the sea again) supported by a powerful, subtle, inexhaustible element which determines what they can do and be—not restrictively but as a bare matter of fact. And when we recognise that such and such a strategy simply doesn't fit with what is human in God's eyes, we don't seek to limit some abstract freedom—only to remind ourselves that we can be only what we can be. The freedom to abandon children, to forget any claims of fidelity in relationships (from sex to ordinary promise keeping), to abuse the environment with impunity, to enslave or torture—these cannot be reconciled with justice in the biblical sense, and so, from the perspective of Exodus, they cannot be real freedoms. They are part of the slavery of fantasy.

Just as with Genesis, the good news is that, since God is unalterably the way God is, there are things about our world and ourselves that no hostile or oppressive power can ever destroy, however hard they try. The apparent inflexibility of the just and lawgiving God is in fact the most profound guarantee of a human dignity which is indestructible. An alleluia for exodus is a thanksgiving for this connection between the utter consistency of God and the gift God gives of forming a society which reflects in human terms something of that divine dependability. And if we start asking about our current societies what degree of dependability they show, we might come up with some sobering answers. The mantras of maximising freedom in various contexts have regularly been an excuse for moving that bit further from a social order that commands trust. When we eagerly set out to export our freedoms to other societies, it is at least worth asking whether we have any understanding of biblical liberty and its uncompromising commitment to the life and security and creativity of the other, the neighbour.

It all helps us see why the offer of freedom in Exodus's terms doesn't invariably strike the slave as good news any more than it does the slave owner. To be free on these terms is to accept a task, not to be relieved of all labour; it is to accept God's work, to agree to swim on his tides. God's love is, so Genesis showed us, endlessly flexible, finding ways through the spiny thickets of our failures and wrong turnings. Exodus shows the other side of that, a love that is inflexible in that it cannot be or give less than it is, cannot therefore be content with leaving us comfortable, accepting our definitions of what makes us safe or happy.

It is an awkward note to strike in a supposedly relaxed culture. But it also casts some light on the darker side of the exodus story itself. Exodus is celebrated at

Passover; and we can't forget what "Passover" means. The Israelites were spared when the angel of death slaughtered all the firstborn of Egypt as a prelude to the release of the slaves. We can't leave Exodus without giving some thought to this shocking narrative. Is the God we have met in Genesis, the God who will give law and justice in Exodus, a God who can be held responsible for the killing of innocent men, women, and children because of their race, as the story might imply?

No one can know what memory or tradition lies behind this story, but I think we have got it very wrong if we suppose that this reveals in God an arbitrary and bloodthirsty element. The scholars have always recognised the problem. And insofar as there is a solution, it is connected with this not always easy or welcome sense of the divine inflexibility. We saw earlier how the coming of unqualified love is a matter of terror to some. Because God cannot be less than God is, there is no way in which God can make things easy for either the slave or the slave owner. And if your life and identity are bound up with slave owning, what can God's liberating arrival mean but death?

In an obscure way, the story of the angel of death lets us know that liberation comes at a price. For the slave owner, losing what he owns feels like the worst possible assault on who he is. But the point is that God's justice is for him too. As long as he is a slave owner, he is not free. Yet again, in another not very well-known passage, St. Augustine captures the heart of it: the soul of the tyrant, he says, is destroyed by his tyranny just as much as the body of those over whom he tyrannises. The tyrant is liberated by whatever stops him being a tyrant. It will wrench his very being; but the inflexibility of God cannot make it easy. And because the slave so often has an investment in the security of slavery, she too will feel that wrenching of the soul, a death of sorts. The darkness of the Passover night is what both oppressor and oppressed have to live through if they are to be in the company of the liberating God. He cannot be less than he is; and so there is in his company that moment of breakage and terror and death for all that cannot live in proximity to God—which is rather a lot of what we take for granted in our lives.

The new creation, unlike the first creation, does not come into being without this. Genesis sets its face firmly against all the creation myths of the ancient world—a divine creator struggling against chaos in a sort of cosmic drama. The drama is here, in Exodus; because creation has become so deeply lost and alienated from itself, its restoration comes with upheaval and pain. The act of creation itself is not a mythical battle or even a mythical birth, but liberation demands that sort of language. For us to be changed, to be set in new relationships with God and each other, for justice to be done, there is no avoiding cost.

We may well hesitate before singing any easy alleluias at this point. We cannot praise God for the deaths of innocent others. There is an old rabbinic story of the angels rejoicing before God as the Egyptians drown in the Red Sea, only to be rebuked by God: "My children the Egyptians lie dead, and you sing and dance?" Can we praise God for death in ourselves, the death of the spirit of slavery, the death of both the slave and the slave owner in our own hearts? We should be able to. But the story seems to say that it is not our own courageous suffering that wins the day. And we fall victim to all sorts of illusion if we indulge in any heroics over that. We may know or trust that the spirit of slavery is being put to death in us, but it was not our initiative that set this in motion. We are not equipped to bear very much reality, as the poet said.

So when freedom and truth come into the world, why is the world not destroyed by the contact? No one can see God and live, Exodus tells us. If the angel of divine presence kills the dearest objects of the love of the slave owners, why not the slaves too, the friends as well as the enemies, since God cannot be less than God? Exodus has given us grounds for alleluias over its affirmation of God's liberty as it shares itself with us. Does it also prepare the ground for another and deeper and more difficult alleluia about how the cost of freedom is actually borne?

Growing into the Unknown

FRIDAY

One of the undoubted gifts to the world from the Jewish-Christian tradition is the weekend. Plenty of cultures have carved up time into seven-day portions (it's a convenient way of dividing the lunar month), but only our own tradition has marked out days of rest in quite this way. And thanks to the dual roots of Western civilisation, both Saturday and Sunday can be counted as rest days, the Jewish Sabbath and the Christian Lord's Day.

No wonder, then, that Friday has a particular sort of feel to it. Schoolteachers both dread and long for Friday afternoon; if they are wise and want to avoid mayhem, they won't schedule anything too demanding for the children. Businesses declare Friday a dressing-down day. People walk around wearing T-shirts with the message, "Thank God it's Friday" (or some more robust version of the same idea). Friday is the time for winding down, getting ready to relax; the week is fading away.

Christians may well have mixed feelings about this. Friday commemorates the anguish and death of Christ on the cross; historically it's a day of fasting—the one bit of traditional discipline that a lot of people (not just Catholics) vaguely recall is that you're supposed to eat fish on Fridays. Weekly patterns of liturgical worship always give to Friday a theme connected with Christ's death. It isn't exactly a relaxing theme to reflect upon, a day to be greeted with a sigh of relief.

But there is something in common between the Friday of popular culture and all that surrounds Good Friday. People who usually observe Good Friday in church will recognise the feeling that comes at the end of a long service or a Three Hours Devotion. Just as with ordinary human bereavement, there is a point of simple exhaustion. The tears have been shed, the calls have been made, the arrangements are in hand; now what do I do? It seems a bit wrong just to sit in front of the television, but what else is there? The world is empty and grey, nothing much seems worth doing, and I can't muster the energy for anything fresh. And so, at the end of a Good Friday service, there is always a muted feeling, sometimes expressed in the way a service ends; in the Catholic and Anglican rites for the day, you're told to leave without ceremony at the end—no processions or stirring final hymn. The church is stripped of its decoration, and you go out in that sort of "grey" atmosphere, tired and rather numb.

Years ago, an older priest, a very austere and frighteningly perceptive man, asked me what I did when I'd finished preaching a Three Hours Devotion (one of the more draining exercises the clergy have to undertake). I ummed and aahed a bit, and he came to my rescue by saying that he usually went to the cinema. It was a relief to hear someone come clean about it; when all has been said on Good Friday, when you have sat and tried to focus on the cross for all that time, there's no point in pretending to be "religious" any longer. Just face the tiredness and the emptiness, and slump.

It's not quite the comfortable self-indulgence of the end of the working week. But it does acknowledge that the moment comes when you can't even try, and you just have to let go and stop struggling. Not that Good Friday is about *your* heroic efforts of piety and self-sacrifice—anything but. Just that the enormous scale of what's been transacted and recalled exhausts your resources for speaking and feeling. It's simply too big. Sometimes theological experts have commented on the great Passions of Bach that they end without a word about the Resurrection hope; their final choruses are all to do with rest and sleep and twilight. But the theological experts don't always understand that you can't hurry the Resurrection. There has to be that dead time when the reality of loss, the seriousness of the story you've been reenacting, can sink in. I'm always grateful for that sudden slackening on Good Friday which allows me to live in a bit of an emotional limbo for a while. The greatest struggle in the world's history is over, and all I can ever think or say about it will be inadequate to the reality. That's all right, says God, I don't ask for your emotions at screaming pitch; sit still and breathe deeply for a while. It's all been done; the arrangements have been made.

It's never been entirely easy for Christians to find the right words for Good Friday. Sometimes they have indeed tried to stoke the emotions in an unreal or manipulative way. And the theories that we have elaborated to help us make sense of the event have often fallen over their own feet in unhelpful complexity. All we need to know is that, as one of the simplest and best-loved hymns for the day says, "It was for us / He hung and suffered there," and that, in the words of another hymn, "Love so amazing, so divine / Demands my soul, my life, my all." What can we say? That this event is a gift to us, a gift of such scale and importance that nothing compares with it.

We were thinking a little while back about how humanity bears the cost of meeting God; how can humans encounter God and live? Good Friday is part of the answer, the very strange answer, that Christian belief offers to that question. God has formed a human life that is completely at one with him, completely expressive of who God is; there is in this life no barrier of fear or ignorance between the human mind and the eternal love that sustains and saturates it. This is a life that can stand before God without that terror of annihilation that shadows our approaches to our maker. And the lives that are drawn into the company of that one unshadowed life are given a share in the confidence and intimacy that is found there.

That's a start; but it is not the whole picture, because all of that could be true without Good Friday. So we say more. As we've seen, the holiness of Jesus draws out the violent unholiness of human beings. Much as we might want to be at home with this love, we also dread it and try to push it away. We make ourselves more vulnerable than ever to the fearful strangeness of God's perfection. In the traditional language of the church, we bring our sinfulness fully into the light as we seek to annihilate Jesus, to drive him out of the world he has unsettled and menaced by his enacting of divine love. We drive him into the darkness, the pain, the hell that we (rightly) fear when we approach God or God approaches us.

In a very cramped shorthand, we can say that he suffers what we fear to suffer and deserve to suffer. And because he is who he is, the life of God in flesh and blood, his humanity emerges from that hellish darkness intact and active, still proclaiming and making real the love which it embodies. He has dealt with the cost of liberation and paid the consequences of human revolt. As a human being he has walked into the fire of God's presence and lived. As a divine being he has walked into the fire of human violence and untruth and lived. On Good Friday, those two fires meet, indistinguishable, on the cross: it seems as though sinful humanity is being devoured, destroyed, by the holiness of God and as though loving divinity is being annihilated by the violence of humanity. But as the fire dies down, and the grey world reappears, we begin to know that now there is nothing left in the universe that can take any further the encounter of God and humanity. The extremes have met.

And the world is still there, and we are still there, baffled and stunned and not knowing what to say. At this moment, as Jesus dies and is taken down from the cross, we don't know quite what is to follow. Like the first disciples of Jesus, we may feel as if we don't yet know what has happened. And perhaps with our minds we never fully will. I have just given you a condensed and probably hopelessly confused account of what *might* be said, or one of many things that might be said, but I know quite well that I am already unhappy with what it doesn't and can't say. So I'm grateful that, on Friday, I can stand back for a bit; something has been transacted, I've witnessed something that must surely make a difference, but for now, never mind if the words won't come. Alleluia for this moment when I can rest and wait, without expectation, for whatever may arrive. T. S. Eliot, in his *Four Quartets*, speaks of the point where you have to "Wait without hope/For hope would be hope for the wrong thing." Perhaps these words, more than anything, express that odd moment of Good Friday limbo.

And of course in the Gospel story and in the Jewish world, what happens next is the Sabbath. It's not only that, after the death of Jesus, no one knows what to do; there's nothing that can be done anyway, as everyone gets ready for the day of rest and celebration. Once again, we catch the echo of what the ordinary weekend now feels like—but with a rather fuller set of associations. The numbness and exhaustion of that Friday space of bereavement is taken up into the day on which we remember God's rest, God looking out at the work he has done and finding it very good. The Sabbath for Judaism is not a gap in a busy life but a welcome guest, a chance to share God's vision of the world; be quiet, stop working to justify your existence, and you will be free to see that what God has done is good. In the context of Good Friday, it's an invitation to look at the finished drama of God's encounter with human evil and slavery and say—whether or not we have any idea just how it all works—"so be it"; it's good, and I accept it, however much it challenges and bewilders me.

What did the friends of Jesus and the mother of Jesus think as they lit the Sabbath candles? We don't know if already at that time they spoke—as later Jews were to do and still do—of the Sabbath as a bride coming in beauty and splendour to the house. Perhaps it felt bitterly ironic, so that it was impossible to celebrate; but perhaps also there were moments of feeling that this time of quiet had been given to look back on the horrors of the day and begin to see a little with God's eyes, to see something *finished*, as Jesus himself had cried from the cross. Not yet in any easy sense a good story, not yet a story that could be thought about without heartbreak and guilt and anger, but the end of a life whose integrity had never wavered, a life in which God had continued to come through. And now there is the Sabbath to let it sink in.

Alleluia for Friday, and so alleluia for the Sabbath too. Friday evening, when the Sabbath begins, is still the high point of the week for observant Jews, and those of us who have been fortunate enough to share a Sabbath eve meal with Jewish friends know what an extraordinary time it is. As the prayers are said, the images pour in upon each other—creation and exodus and the temple and the days of the Messiah and the promised return to the Holy Place; as if everything that mattered about being Jewish was coming together. The Sabbath as it arrives tells people that God's time has come—that this is how God spends time with his people, in the breaking of bread and the sharing of joy. Think again of the friends of Jesus on that Sabbath eve. They will have remembered the previous night—ages before, centuries before, as it must have seemed—when Jesus had broken bread and promised to share the cup with them as they drank the new vintage in God's kingdom. As they entered God's time on that Friday night, were they able to receive it as a gift in which to sit silently with the events of the crucifixion?

Normally I don't like speculating about what people in the Gospels "may" or "must" have felt. But it's hard in this case not to. Those disciples cannot but have brought to that Sabbath an almost unmanageable load of images and memories and words and feelings, and I find it impossible not to imagine that God used that Sabbath to prepare something of what they would be facing on Sunday. There is time for the sense of bereavement; there is time for sitting with the bewilderment; there is time also, quite simply, for God. Sunday when it came was, according to all the Gospels, a powerful shock. But perhaps something begins to germinate in that silence.

No ordinary weekend, indeed. An alleluia for Friday is rather different from "Thank God it's Friday." It's not that we're now let off serious thought or action for a couple of days, but that God is giving us space for the greatest work of all, the entry into newness that comes with the Resurrection story. This is healing time, not just time for the engine to idle without purpose. Yet we should be careful not to approach the world's weekend with superiority. The last thing we ought to be doing is badgering overworked people and trying to make them feel bad about relaxing. What I think we should be trying to communicate is two things. One is simply that our leisure time is a gift—but a gift that we might use not just to be completely passive but for ideas and understandings and feelings to germinate, for the world to become deeper as we look at it. And part of the world we look at is the history that contains the record of Jesus and his death. So a second question is whether in our more "spacious" moments we can turn our eyes to that haunting and disturbing story once in a while and ask what it is about it that made so many see it as a turning point, a pivot on which human history swings around.

Space and silence are indeed the conditions for our minds changing and growing. We all know the strange way in which problems rearrange themselves while we're not thinking about them, how names we've forgotten suddenly come up from our unconscious when we have struggled for ages to recover them with our efforts at active recollection. Space is given us, time when we don't have to make our mark and succeed, so that the whole world may slowly rearrange itself around us. So this bridge between Friday and Sabbath is a moment not only of tiredness and disorientation but also of fertility, creativity. If we can turn (I promise for the last time) to the disciples on that first Good Friday, perhaps we can imagine them sitting apart in their diverse kinds of silence—Mary's appalled grief for the child of her body, Peter's incredulous despair at his betrayal, the Beloved Disciple's mind weaving in an almost dreamlike way, back and forth among the images and echoes of the previous twenty-four hours—and letting each other be. The fertility is also a matter of solitude, leaving room for one another.

Thank God it's Friday. The working week is over. Our working week, so that we have a Sabbath to greet and celebrate, a time that is just God's time; and also God's working week—the days of creation, which have at last come to a pause as the labour of the new creation is finished. Because of what has happened on the cross, in that fiery mystery we so struggle to get our minds around, the time has arrived when God and humanity can sit together—not yet knowing quite how to talk to each other, it seems, just being in the same space. Something unfamiliar, but not exactly (as it might have been) frightening.

When we feel helpless and inarticulate about what God is like or what God is doing, that can be a hugely positive thing, a way of being reminded that the focus for the language of faith isn't us and our thoughts and feelings but God. The Friday gift is in its own way a recall to the gifts of Genesis and Exodus—the vision of a God immeasurably beyond what we can manage or grasp, who is what and who he is in freedom and joy. If we sit silent and drained under the cross, perhaps wishing we could say or think something appropriately devout, something fitting to the occasion, we can hear God saying, "I am who I am; and that's why the words aren't there, for you or any created being." And, remembering the liberating story that begins from those words in Exodus, we may well lift our heads and hearts and cry out, from those tired and hoarse throats, an alleluia for Friday, its darkness and its hidden promises.

DEATH

Death, the spectre that broods over every morning, hiding around the edges of the day, standing just outside the boundaries of the present moment, has been a constant companion in my life. First my father went, a figure largely unknown to a child of three, but present for that very reason perhaps every day of my life thereafter. Thanks to him, death, the notion that things die, go, leave us despite their care for us or ours for them, became part of the fabric of my life.

The progression of losses after that took on more of the routine: old grandparents, sick uncles, and tired old aunts shriveled up and faded away, sadly but understandably. These were deaths that were within the natural order of things, where people died in rank and other people filled in the spaces.

Then two things happened. First, a little girl with whom I rode the bus to school stepped in front of it one day and was crushed under its wheels. I remember her parents, ashen-faced, stunned, standing there over her dead body like ghosts themselves. But most of all I remember the size of the coffin. It was too small, I thought, to hold so big a thing as death.

Finally, I remember the sudden death of a best friend, thrown from the back seat of a car in fog, unfound for hours, gone in midair.

It was true, I knew now. Life, hard hewn and slowly shaped, can change in seconds. Nothing is secure; nothing is permanent; aloneness is just around the corner. But why?

What's to thank God for in cases like this where nothing seems to take the pattern we devise for it: no father as you grow, no family as you age, no friend as faithful companion as you explore the world around you?

How do we deal with the deaths and losses we cannot possibly explain? When the old "God in the sky" images finally give way to more adult awareness, what is left? How can anyone possibly say thank you, alleluia, God be praised for this?

The kind of death we see as the end of everything does not really exist. We just think it does. We simply fear it does. What will happen to me, our heart wails beneath the rhythm of the daily, if he dies or she is taken from me or this ends or that disappears? What will be left for me? How can I possibly survive? How will I ever go on?

Death may, of course, be the trigger of despair. But death is also the answer to despair. Once we have known death, up close and personal, despair can barely touch us again. Death teaches us that my life only ends when it ends.

The fact is that we do go on after those around us die: soldiers on the field beside us drop on both sides of us, friends in the same car crash that barely touches me are killed by the same impact, family members stricken by family diseases all go, but we remain. We wake to an empty dawn on the one hand, and a new invitation to life at the same time. Death is an alleluia moment of immense proportions. Thank God for the lives that were, we now realize with terrible awareness, but thank God for our own new life as well. Bleak as it may seem at the present time, unwanted as it is, perhaps, it is, nevertheless, here. Death is a turn in a road we did not imagine, but the road goes always in the same place it always has: toward the coming to life of the rest of me.

Death brings losses that are actually another kind of gain. I must choose now whether to give in to the death of the spirit or to take on the rebirth of myself. Those whose first loves die live to love again. Those for whom death has been the end of one kind of life are given the opportunity to know another. Those who hoarded every moment, every penny, every bit of stable and secure routine learn that, having nothing, it is still possible to have everything there is that is worth having: an awareness of the beautiful, a love of the good, a new sense of what is true in life.

Loss is clearly not the only side of death. There is newness to be praised in death as well.

Change is the facet of death that brings with it the challenge to be more than I ever knew I was. Change brings an alleluia for the reservoir of hidden strength that wells up only at the point when all I know of myself is total weakness.

For those for whom the very thought has been paralyzing, death catapults us into an orbit of transitions. We must begin to talk to new people, go new places, change addresses and phone numbers and homes. We find ourselves stretched beyond ourselves, left open to the elements, confronted by another face of God in other places and other people. We are borne along on angels' wings by angels we never recognized before emptiness swallowed us up and left us to find other ways through the day.

Unlike plans and strategies, goals and steps along the way, change simply deposits us in places we never planned to be, in order to show us all the other sides of life we've missed while we were bedding down inside a Fabergé egg of our own design. Change teaches us that life is an exercise of melting into eternity. It is not a process of control to be engineered with only our security in mind. Change throws us open to the universe in a giddy kind of free fall that teaches us faith, that exercises our trust. Say alleluia to the changes that free you from the predictable.

There is a perspective that comes from loss and change, from death and endings, that can be gotten no other way. Death changes the landscape of both the present and the future. It enables us, sometimes for the first time in life, to see the things we too often miss: the value of time, the richness of fun, the balm of talk, the rarity of intimacy, the measure of enough.

Death has something to do with the way we measure importance in days to come. Suddenly, when what is really basic to our lives is gone, everything we thought was really major to it shrinks in size, takes its place among the routine and the humdrum, the inflated and the distorted things of life. We find, in death, that suddenly the work and the money, the neighborhood and the new car, the promotion and the title begin to pale. Perspective sets in and we begin to see more clearly now. Sometimes it is only in darkness that we can begin to see the light.

Then, from the vantage point of death, with a truer, sharper set of calipers, we can begin to measure one of our judgments against another, one of our values against another, one of our decisions against another. We begin the process of review that comes with the questions, Now what is my life about? Now what do I believe? Now what do I wish I had done? Now which direction shall I take and what of my old self shall I take with me when I do?

Then I begin to get ready for my own death. Then I decide, in the face of a loved one lost, what kind of person I myself want to be at the moment all the moments end. One of the arch-definitions of fulfillment in all of scripture occurs when, after years of separation, Jacob sees his lost son Joseph in Egypt. In a burst of emotion, Jacob records what his whole life has really been about. Jacob, scripture reports, simply says, "Now that I know that you live, I can die." Death makes all of us ask ourselves what our life has really been about: achievement, status, security—or the securing of a better world for others. Death asks us what we want to have become of our lives before we die. What, death says, will be the alleluia of your own life?

Then comes growth, death's final gift. We find ourselves different than we were before death confronted us with our limits, prodded us toward new possibilities, gave us a new look at life and all its little pieces, made us choose again for the lasting beyond the ephemeral.

Then the alleluia of death becomes the alleluia of growth into everything we were ever meant to be.

So alleluia to the early loss of a young father. Without that death my life would never have developed as it did. Alleluia for the death of a childhood companion. Without that death I might never have realized so young that life is not forever. And alleluia for the death of a friend whose energy and strength is a light for my path even yet, frozen in time, never weary, always prodding me on. Thanks to all of them, I have found new things where I thought nothing would ever be again. I got a chance to look at life anew. I began to think more carefully about what counts and what doesn't. I have grown beyond my own narrow limits to a world much broader than myself. I have come to understand, I think, what Jean Paul Richter meant when he wrote "Winter, which strips the leaves from around us / makes us see the distant regions they formerly concealed." Indeed.

Future

I remember the conversations so well, all of them. They each spoke of a time not yet and a life not lived. But they spoke as well of a time of hope, of remembering again that life presses on to a point unseen where life is meant to be fuller and more fulfilling at the same time.

In every case just the thought of the future itself was enough to stop thought as well as to start it. Future, it seems, is the unseen magnet of life before which we all stand helpless and impotent.

"If George Bush gets reelected," the woman said, "I don't know how I can stay in this country. I don't know what I'll do." Here, for one woman at least, was the unwanted future at its starkest. The present was frustrating; the unknown future was troubling. For this woman the whole concept of society and government and citizenry was now at stake. The future for her would demand determining if even issues as great as the political, the social, the global are the real essence of life.

And if they are, what does the future demand when you lose them? Do we simply stay in place and see what will happen in it all? Or must we make changes now to guard against the days to come?

"I'm taking the state boards over again, " the young man said. "If I don't pass them this time, my life will be over." Here was the feared future with all its bleakness, all its despair. For this young man, life was a funnel that led to one place and one place only. The future for him would lie in deciding whether what he wanted to do with his life was also doable some other way.

"I'm going to divinity school," the woman said. "I don't know if I'll get a parish, but I intend to try. Then whatever happens, happens." Here was the future unsure but bright and full of purpose. The future for this woman lay in her willingness to go into it light-footed and full of heart. For her the future was not defined or carved in stone; it was a place of possibilities only. The future meant the freedom to explore life with all its many starting points and divergences along the way until all together they finally became the life she was meant to lead. She would recognize it when she got there.

"I'm not in the right place and I realize it," the man said, "but I don't know where I really want to be." Here was the future greyed out and unwelcoming. The future for this man involved looking within himself for some kind of interest and some sense of talent to take him there. Future, in this case, has something to do with sorting out all his past attempts to find a home in the universe with an eye to discovering what it was that was missing still.

Clearly, future is many things at once. It is the vessel into which we pour all our hopes and all our fears. "When all else is lost," Christian Bovee says, "the future still remains." The problem is that future is a panacea for some and a threat to others. It is at the edge of the future that we walk off the side of a cliff into the arms of God.

The spiritual challenge of the future resides in being able to accept it before we know it.

But accepting the future before we know what it is becomes one of the central problems of life. Rather than embrace the unknown, we stumble along from one fear to another. From day to day, intent on going tenderly into the future we want for ourselves, we are inclined to do one of two things: escape the present or cast it in stone.

So we cling and claw our way from day to day, trying to preserve this, to avoid that, intent on our need to control tomorrow and awash in our uncertainties along the way. Then we begin to see what the future really demands of us. We come to realize that it is not the particulars, the details of time and place and position to which the future finally takes us that really matter much. No, it isn't so much what happens to us in the future that counts. It is the attitudes we take to it that make all the difference between a future that's full and a future that's frustrating.

After all, Charles Colson went through a prison sentence and came out into a completely different future than he had ever imagined—and thrived in it. Christopher Reeves, Superman, became a paralyzed man who fought depression for two years and, before it was over, became more effective, better known, and more socially involved than he had ever been before the accident that everyone was sure had destroyed his life. A friend of mine lost his wife from hepatitis three days after they took her to the hospital. He was left with five children under the age of twelve and went through five brain operations after that. Is he happy? He says he is. As John Lennon put it, "Life is what happens to you while you're busy making other plans."

The function of the future must be, then, not simply the achievement of the goals and dreams of the present. The function of the future is to keep us growing beyond our own small designs for ourselves in the present.

The future, because it is the unknown factor in every life, calls us to live with untried courage always. The philosopher Alfred North Whitehead in his great sweeping analysis of human history wrote about civilization in general: "All centuries are dangerous, it is the business of the future to be dangerous. It must be admitted that there is a degree of instability which is inconsistent with civilization. But, on the whole, the great ages have been the unstable ages."

Whitehead's meaning is clear: Without a modicum of order and predictability the whole enterprise of human and institutional development would be impossible. And yet, on the whole, the great ages have been those in which the old routines and ideas, the organizational predictables and the moral imperatives broke down and the barely imaginable of the last generation became the commonplace of the new. Then life as we had never known it broke through the old borders of the mind and the world became fresh again.

It is precisely those unstable eras of our own lives that make or break us, too. They bring great changes to bear on us. They draw greatness out of us. They demand of us the holy audacity to believe that, having dealt with the past, I am equal to the future as well.

Today I can handle, I know. Tomorrow may ask something of me that I have never been called to give before this. I am not prepared for it; I am simply there. But every new day I cope with well is another exercise in a courage I did not know I had.

When the spiritual question becomes what is the purpose of an unknown future, why are we not be able to see what's coming and prepare for it, the answer must be that only the willingness to face the future can call us to become a part of ourselves we did not realize we still needed to become.

The future is what brings a person to full stature when it is so easy to crawl into the cocoon of what we've always been and hide from the demands of life to do more—to raise the baby alone, to realize that we are more than our physical bodies, to adjust to new times and new places and new people and new threats to our psyche and our very soul.

In all this, the future is the only sure proof of faith we'll ever have. Faith is the willingness to believe that, however dark the present, God's future means only good for us. It is the challenge to a Muslim detainee in Guantanamo Bay to believe that, in the end, God will sustain and God will justify. It is the challenge to a young American soldier in Iraq to have the courage not to become what war creates—mad and mean and inhumane—whatever the fears and the pressures. It is the challenge to the survivors to believe that God will raise us all from this valley of the dead to live again.

But that requires that the future give its gift—the willingness to make whatever effort the future requires.

It is the willingness to make whatever effort it takes to make the future whole and holy that is the antidote to the depression that comes with fear and lack of control and uncertainty. Only the future confronts us with having to make a choice between life and death, between living life to the fullest and curling up into a fetal position and saying, "I quit."

The future is the call to the desert of life through which we all must pass before the desert can bloom in us.

An alleluia to the future is an alleluia to the courage and faith and effort it will take to wring out of us every last drop of character, every ounce of faith, every trembling "yes" we've ever said to the God of surprises.

It was an alleluia to the future that John the Baptist brought to the world. In the face of total confusion and complete unclarity and absolute uncertainty about who this Jesus was, John the Baptist went on speaking his truth and pointing out to others what he knew in his heart he had been born to proclaim. The rest he left to God.

Singing alleluia to the future is the way we embrace the imminent and leave it to God at the same time.

In the meantime, Henry Ward Beecher assures us, there is only one real task in life: "No matter what looms ahead, if you can eat today, enjoy the sunlight today, mix good cheer with friends today, enjoy it and bless God for it. Do not look back on happiness—or dream of it in the future. You are only sure of today; do not let yourself be cheated out of it."

Darkness

Somewhere along the line, the woman I once adored left me. I was her star, her joy, her best companion, her confidante, her only child. My mother and I were more like sisters, more like friends, than we were mother and daughter. She told me everything. I lied to her only once.

When my stepfather didn't want me to start dating I told them both that I was going to a movie with girlfriends and then met the boy on a corner somewhere. She figured it all out, however, and, instead of cutting me out of the warm circle of her trust, let my stepfather know in no uncertain terms that insisting on unnatural absolutes was exactly what would "make a liar out of me." After that the rule became that boys were to come to the house first—before I went out with them—for the regular parental review. And she and I went back to telling one another the truth. About boys. About life. About everything.

I expected we would have long and happy years together. I actually planned for them. When my stepfather died, leaving her a relatively young widow, I was sure we'd go places together now, and celebrate everything together, and work together on the projects that had become my concentration.

But, little by little, the relationship began to go awry. She got edgy and testy and irritated. She didn't do the things she promised she would. I'd go for her shopping list and it wasn't made out yet. I'd squeeze in a trip to take her to the bank and when we got there she didn't have her bank book. She began to complain about everything—about the places I'd take her for Mother's Day, about the things I was doing, about the people I liked.

Then one day, she began accusing me of making phone calls to her—and hanging up when she answered.

I began to avoid going to the house. We were strangers now. This was a woman I had never known.

It was years before they began to call it "Alzheimer's disease." By then I was full of anger. After that, I was full of guilt. She lived for twenty-eight years with the disease, and so did I.

It was a long, dark time but, I began to realize later, it was not a useless time. There were even reasons, I discovered later, for alleluias here.

Darkness is that period of life when nothing seems to be going as we expected. We find ourselves derailed in our journey to our dreams, not only by things we didn't foresee but by things we simply could not have imagined. When we see trouble coming, that is not darkness. That is the inevitable, plain as day, sure as tomorrow. What we can see coming is simply a problem to be solved. What we cannot see coming is a shock to be endured. It is disorientation. The world shifts on its axis and tilts us with it—all our hopes, all our expectations, all our certainties.

Darkness consumes and envelops us. It also makes us look at life all over again. Whatever we once took for granted, darkness makes us rethink, reevaluate, relinquish.

The value of a dark time is that it insists that we become new, even to ourselves. I was no longer the darling daughter of a doting mother. I was alone in the world, at best, abandoned for nothing I could imagine. By doing what I had always done, being what I had always been, I had done something wrong. But who knew what? Or why? Or how to repair it? It was time to find within myself the resources that the once apparently unalterable refuge of motherhood had once provided. I began to redefine myself, to feel the strength that comes with knowing that you are enough for you.

Darkness is a time of beginning again. We are forced then to determine a new way to be in the world. It is a frightening time—but a liberating time as well. It gives us the opportunity to make new choices about life, about relationships, about our dreams and our plans. It tells us that the old world has passed away and the new one is of our making.

In a busy world we seldom get the luxury of reviewing where we are. We simply get up every morning and go on. Yesterday becomes today and every day thereafter. Now when all the past decisions and relationships are in flux, we are required to review them all. How will we deal with them next? What questions will we ask of each of them? How will we determine what to do with each of them?

It is a very spiritual time. It is a time that challenges us to recreate ourselves in the image of the Spirit who calls us to become everything we can be. The darkness that blocks us from becoming is the very womb of a new life.

There is another dimension to darkness that seldom comes at any other time of life. It is the question of choice. In darkness we forget: we really have two choices. We can go on as is. Or we can go on differently. I could have collapsed with the loss of my mother as I knew her. The feeling was real. The situation was true. How could I possibly simply call my mother dead in my mind? After all, she wasn't dead. And, it seemed, she had suddenly —no, slowly—begun to hate me and everything I did. How could I possibly simply forget her and go on?

But I did. Yes, something had happened to our relationship. Yes, I mourned her deeply. No, I couldn't seem to improve the situation. Therefore there was nothing I could do but cut the emotional bonds and go on—and stand by at the same time. And I did. It was years before there was a word—Alzheimer's—for the situation, but by that time it was too late. I was alone. We were estranged. She no longer recognized me.

Would I do it differently now, in an era when there is so much data that describes the disease and its likely effects? Of course I would. But then, that is not darkness; that is disease. In the period in which I dealt with the condition it was the loss of a relationship, the pernicious erosion of a relationship I wanted and could not have.

The message in the darkness did not come immediately. The meaning came only a few years before the final burial of a soul that had died long years before.

To succumb to darkness, to fail to trust the light that is coming when this period is over, is therefore to fail to trust the continuing new dawns of life.

But if we can possibly learn to trust darkness, to understand that life is a pattern of starts and stops, of celebrating the past, of coming to terms with the present, of believing the future to be kind, then we can come to understand that the dark parts are only those closing-down moments, like flowers at night, till the sun shines once more.

Darkness signals a change point in life. It is Lot wailing in Sodom about having to leave the place while God has in store for him a whole new world.

Darkness deserves gratitude. It is the alleluia point at which we learn to understand that all growth does not take place in the sunlight. Then we come to understand that God is at work in our lives even when we believe that nothing whatsoever is going on.

My mother died in my arms in my own monastery, at peace, happy, well cared for, and safe. And I became ready to face the world all by myself, without a mother, without a community, with nothing, if necessary, because I had already learned how to be alone. Alleluia.

God

After weeks of nonstop bombing by the German air force, a story came out of the London blitz during World War II that, though certainly apocryphal, makes the point of how it feels to be a person alone in the universe. "And Dear God," the child ended his litany of nightly blessings, "Please take care of yourself because if anything happens to you, we're all sunk."

The notion of the presence of God in life is a mystical one. It does not rely for its authenticity on mathematical equations or test tube analyses or even on logical propositions, many of which could do as much to prove that God does not exist as that God does. In fact, theological propositions themselves, in proving God to be male, for instance, and the earth to be the center of the universe, have been notoriously in error. Better to use spiritual instinct on this one, perhaps, than to rely on human intelligence to authenticate a divine proposition.

So the question comes up over and over again: If God exists, God must be good. But how can a good God allow so much suffering and do nothing to stop it? If God cannot stop it, the argument goes on, then God cannot be God. And if God can stop it, but does not, then God cannot be good.

When the Indonesian tsunami of December 2004 hurled a thirty-foot wall of water against eleven countries in fifteen minutes' time, wiping out whole villages, drowning over two hundred thousand people, the question exploded into the middle of the publishing world.

The preoccupation with the question raised a kind of theological tsunami of its own. Every newspaper and magazine, from one end of the world to the other, published articles purporting to answer the question.

These were publications, remember, that reported regularly on space probes to the moon, Mars, and Saturn. These were reporters who had seen the obliteration of Hiroshima and Nagasaki by one small atomic bomb each. These were big-city newspapers whose newsrooms were fed by the nanosecond from computers around the world. These were sophisticates in a technological world, all asking the same questions: Where was God now? Why had God allowed such destruction of the innocent? How could a good God stand by and allow such a thing to happen?

Not since the Lisbon earthquake in 1755 and the loss of a city of innocents had there been such an outpouring of God-talk about a natural disaster. There, on the brink of the Enlightenment and its growing awareness that natural causes trigger natural events, the question of the function of God in the universe became central. The God of magic acts and human puppetry, the philosophers agreed over time, was dead.

Since then earthquakes killing thousands of people everywhere have happened regularly but few, if any, questioned those events. Hurricanes wiped whole villages off mountainsides and no one collapsed in paroxysms of doubt or horror or despair. Yet now the question of God's goodness, if newspapers are any measure of genuine popular interest, had emerged again with a vengeance.

But it was the wrong question.

The question is not, Where was God in the midst of such a disaster? God was exactly where God was when Job's friends, in the face of the collapse of his health, his wealth, and his reputation demanded that Job ask, too, how is it that the good suffer and God does nothing about it. Clearly God, the life force behind all life, was allowing that life, both human and natural, to proceed as it was made, naturally and unrestrained. It was that simple.

No, the question is not, How can a good God allow such a thing?

The question is, Why praise a God like this? Why sing alleluia to the God of tsunamis and earthquakes, of war and death, of suffering and pain? Why, indeed?

The answer is almost too obvious to bear. It is the spiritual consciousness that having made the world, having given it everything it needs to continue, having brought it to the point of abundance and possibility and dynamism, God left it for us to finish. God left it to us to be the mercy and the justice, the charity and the care, the righteousness and the commitment, all that it will take for people to bring the goodness of God to outweigh the rest.

The mystic knows both the truth of it and the price of it. It is for us to put on the mind of God that it will take to bring the goodness of God to the evil in the world we see around us.

It is up to us to bring resurrection out of suffering, to bring creativity to what is yet undeveloped.

We pollute our skies, profane our waters, experiment with nuclear explosions in the South Seas and then never even bother to put up early warning systems of seismic activity in an area whose natural processes we may well have violated ourselves.

At the same time, we do not doubt our own right to bring about human destruction and disasters. Those things we call "politics" and "military security" and "foreign policy" and "justice"—and free will. We do not want God interfering for the other side then.

We want God to interfere only on behalf of our convenience, on behalf of our politics, on behalf of our definitions of right. And we call it an assault on our faith when that doesn't happen.

What we cannot control, do not see, cannot understand destroys the idol that is ourselves. Then we find ourselves dealing with holy doubt.

We must begin to doubt, perhaps, that we can do anything we want to do with this globe and get away with it. Australian researchers tell us in a recent issue of the journal *Geology* that the Great Australian Desert, a now uninhabitable two-thirds of the continent, remains that way today because of the kind of burning practiced by its inhabitants fifty thousand years ago.

We must start to doubt that we can go on destroying nature as we know it—its rain forests, and ozone layer, and Great Lakes, and ocean harvests, and top soil—with impunity. Otherwise, when the oceans rise and the islands disappear and the coastlines erode and the fresh waters dry up, we will simply absolve ourselves of the responsibility to be fully human by asking again, Where is God in all of this?

Now that nature has once again had its way with us, perhaps it will finally provoke the alleluia of accountability in us. Maybe we will begin to take responsibility not to control natural disasters but also not to provoke them. Perhaps we will learn to respect them, to cope with them well, to limit their effects, to rescue their victims. Then we will put sensors in the Indian Ocean in order to be able to detect seismic activity. We will see that the poor have more to live in than bamboo houses on the beach. We will build the relief centers we need to care for those who miss the signals or get lost in the water. Then the beaches of the poor will stand as strong as the beaches of the rich, who survive hurricane after hurricane with loss of property but little loss of life.

Then we will know that the alleluia we sing to the God of creation is like the Israelites praising God for giving them the law. We will see, too, that it is the very fact that this good God allows us to respond to evil that brings out the best in us.

Alleluia to the God who requires us to become marble out of clay, to bring everything we can be out of the breath of Nothingness.